Eighteenth Century

Blogosphere

Eighteenth Century Blogosphere

Richard J. Warren

Muddy Pig Press • Las Vegas, Nevada

Photo Credit: fotolia - Morphart

ISBN-13:978-0692337585

ISBN-10: 069233758X

Printed in the United States of America

www.muddypigpress.com

Muddy Pig Press • Las Vegas, Nevada

The French Revolution taught us the rights of man. – Thomas Sankara

Acknowledgements

Creating a book such as this one does not happen in a vacuum, it requires the assistance of many others along the way.

I would like to thank my colleagues, Kristen Gazmen, Spenser Grimes, Diane Ireland, Jenessa Kenway, Cortney Lechmann, Sarah Lyons, Rebecca Noback, Tynelle Olivas, Aisha Ratanapool, Carlie Sanders and Ariel Santos for their support and encouragement.

Special thanks go to University of Nevada Las Vegas professor Dr. Anne Stevens for sharing her knowledge of Eighteenth Century English literature and her suggestions of sources for this project. I would also like to thank Dr. Christopher Decker of UNLV for his input and direction for this project. Without his inspiration this volume would not have been possible...or necessary. Hopefully it is worthy.

As always, I would like to thank the "piglets" at the Muddy Pig Press for their assistance during the publishing process.

Table of Content

Editor's Note

The purpose of this volume is to provide a sampling of essays debating the French Revolution. By providing a selection representing different ages, economic backgrounds and sex it is possible to see how these characteristics may, or may not, have influenced the respective writer's position. This proved to be no easy task.

The decision was made to opt for essays from the most well-known essayists as opposed to the more obscure writer's whose opinions may well have been just as valid. The available essays from Price, Burke, Paine, Young, Godwin and Wollstonecraft are quite lengthy. This necessitated selecting excerpts that would illustrate both the respective writer's style and political leanings.

The comparisons were made of essays written from the beginning of the revolt and ending prior to the Reign of Terror under Robespierre. The opinions of many, though not all, of the writers shifted as the horrors of the end stages of the revolution became known.

Introduction

The internet and its ability to instantaneously transmit information has unleashed a whirlwind of commentary on various topics, not the least of which are political concerns. Issues are examined, debated, attacked and defended by writers with considerable knowledge, experience and expertise as well as by those who are neophytes in the arena of world politics. However, technology has not given birth to such dialogue, it has merely increased the rate at which the discussion takes place.

Revolution was a defining issue of the last quarter of the Eighteenth Century with signature events occurring in both America and France. The French Revolution was particularly troubling for many in England with the overthrow of Louis XVI raising questions about their own system of government. Some supported the French King and Queen while others sided with the rebellious factions. This was likely debated at all levels of English society of the time, but it was a war of words between prominent writers that claimed center stage. A series of exchanges of letters and essays, aptly named the "war of pamphlets," constituted the blogosphere of the Eighteenth

Century. The essayists and letter writers – the bloggers – were representative of different age groups, backgrounds and sex. Like their twenty-first century counterparts, their opinions were shaped by these distinct traits.

The revolution in France was triggered by economic concerns, not the least of which was a poor harvest in 1788 that lead to shortages of bread. Another defining issue was the unfair tax system that favored the nobility at the expense of the poorer members of French society. Common people suffered while the aristocracy seemingly thrived creating an uneasy atmosphere. The King, Louis XVI, was unable to solve the problems but instead added to it with his lavish spending in a time of economic crisis. The unrest grew and led to what is often considered the symbolic start of the revolt – the storming of the Bastille prison by an angry mob on July 14, 1789. Four months later the first salvo of the pamphlet war was fired by Richard Price in November of 1789.

Many other writers would join the debate as the revolution developed. Some took positions in support of the French monarchy while many more assumed an opposing stance. While opinions were apt to change as the reality of the Reign of Terror under Robespierre became known, the early years of the essay exchanges were quite heated. The essays presented here are examined in the order of the author's age rather than the sequence in which they were first published, the intent being to determine whether age was a factor. The background of the writer's is also taken into account. The essayists include two of the elder statesmen in debate, the aforementioned Price and Edmund Burke. Not far removed in age were Thomas Paine and Arthur Young. Younger voices were heard from in William Godwin and the poet William Blake. Not to be forgotten were the women Mary Wollstonecraft and Helen Maria Williams, both fairly young at the time at approximately thirty years of age.

Richard Price was sixty-six years old when he delivered *A Discourse on the Love of Our Country* to the "Society for Commemorating the Revolution in Great Britain" on November 4, 1789. The son of a strict Calvinist minister reputed to have a severe temper, his upbringing may have contributed to the liberal slant he exhibited in his writing (Fowler). Price, himself a Dissenting Unitarian minister, was a supporter of the colonies during the American revolution so it could be expected that he would also support the revolution in France.

Price's essay begins innocently enough with a psalm that he says shows the psalmist's love of his country. He expands on the concept of country to state "by our country is meant, in this case, not the soil or the spot of earth on which we happen to have been born, not the forests and fields, but that community of which we are members" (Price). Referring to a larger community rather than the boundaries of a specific nation is setting the stage for his later assertion that the citizenry has a right to rebel against an unjust government or monarch. The essay says that "a King is no more than the first servant of a republic" and that "His authority is the authority of the community, and the term *Majesty*, which it is usual to apply to him, is by no means his own majesty, but the majesty of the people" (Price). He proceeds to list three principles of the Revolution:

> First, the right to liberty of conscience in religious matters. Secondly, the right to resist power when abused.
> Thirdly, the right to chuse (sic) our own governors, to cashier them for misconduct, and to frame a government for ourselves. (Price)

Price concludes the essay with the call to "Restore to mankind their rights and consent to the correction of abuses, before they and you are destroyed together" (Price). This essay would draw a rebuttal from Sir Edmund Burke.

At sixty-one years of age Burke was only slightly younger than Price at the time his essay, *Reflections on the Revolution in France,* was published. He was born in Ireland, the son of a wealthy lawyer. He received his education at Trinity College in Dublin and while there formed a debate club that later became the College Historical Society and still exists today. His penchant for debate would stay with him throughout his life. A member of Parliament from 1765 to 1794, he supported many liberal causes and was opposed to policies that were harmful to the American colonies. His stance was similar to that of Richard Price in that he was a supporter of the American Revolution. It is somewhat surprising that Burke would swing from the liberal support of the colonies to the conservative stance he exhibited in defense of the French monarchy. Perhaps he couldn't resist a good debate.

Burke is thought to have begun crafting his response shortly after Price delivered his address though it would not be published until November of 1790, a full year later. The essay was written as a "Letter Intended to have been sent to a Gentleman in Paris" and may have begun as a reply to a genuine query requesting his opinion on the events occurring in France. The letter referred to Price as a preacher calling his essay "a very extraordinary miscellaneous sermon" and he made a connection to the English Civil War when he said "That sermon is in a strain which I believe has not been heard in this kingdom, in any of the pulpits which are tolerated or encouraged in it, since the year 1648" (Burke).

Burke assails Price's "gross errors of fact" and the three principles of revolution:

> This new and hitherto unheard-of bill of
> rights, though made in the name of the
> whole people, belongs to those
> gentlemen and their faction only. The

body of the people of England have no share in it. They utterly disclaim it. They will resist the practical assertion of it with their lives and fortunes. (Burke)

Burke believed the British people preferred the status quo and states "We have an inheritable crown, an inheritable peerage, and a House of Commons and a people inheriting privileges, franchises, and liberties from a long line of ancestors" (Burke).

Burke defends the French monarch and, in particular, the Queen. He discussed having seen her about sixteen years earlier:

It is now sixteen or seventeen years since I saw the queen of France, then the dauphiness, at Versailles, and surely never lighted on this orb, which she hardly seemed to touch, a more delightful vision. I saw her just above the horizon, decorating and cheering the elevated sphere she just began to move in—glittering like the morning star, full of life and splendor and joy . (Burke)

Could this infatuation with her image have clouded his opinions concerning the revolution? Having previously been in agreement with Price in regards to the American Revolution it seems odd that he would take such a disparate view of the events in France. The older ages and background do not seem to be a factor in the disagreement between contemporaries Price and Burke.

The middle-aged perspective of Thomas Paine was added to the debate with the publication of *The Rights of Man* in 1791. Though recognizable for his role in the politics of the American revolution, Paine was born in England and lived there until 1774 when, at the age of 37, he moved to America. He lacked the formal education of Price and Burke and began working at the age of thirteen. He endured many hardships including the loss of jobs, failed business venture and the loss of both wife and child during childbirth. His background certainly differed from the previously mentioned essayists and at age 54 he was more than a decade younger than Price.

Paine's essay directly attacks Burke and his defence of the divine right of kings. While Burke asserts there is an "inheritable crown" Paine states "All hereditary government is in its nature tyranny" (Paine). Paine explains further:

> We have heard the Rights of Man
> called a leveling system; but the only
> system to which the word leveling is
> truly applicable, is the hereditary

> monarchical system. It is a system of
> mental leveling. It indiscriminately
> admits every species of character to the
> same authority. Vice and virtue,
> ignorance and wisdom, in short, every
> quality good or bad, is put on the same
> level. Kings succeed each other, not as
> rationals, but as animals. It signifies not
> what their mental or moral characters
> are. (Paine)

Paine goes on to say "what is called monarchy, always
appears to me a silly, contemptible thing" (Paine).

He assails the economic conditions of the time and
links them to the system of government. Paine felt the sting of
poverty and struggle in a way that Price and Burke did not and
this certainly informed his point of view. Where older, and
wealthier, essayists debated the merits of the aristocracy,
Paine questioned the economic distress that necessitated that
the elderly worked and the young all too often found trouble.
Paine stated "When, in countries that are called civilised, we
see age going to the workhouse and youth to the gallows,
something must be wrong in the system of government"
(Paine). He advocated for support of people who have
exceeded their working years and says this "support... is not of
the nature of a charity, but of a right" (Paine). More so than

age, Thomas Paine's position was influenced by his background as a common man.

Several years after Price, Burke and Paine, and after the execution of Louis XVI, Arthur Young, at age fifty-two, wrote *The Example of France, a Warning to Britain.* This 1793 essay followed his work *Travels in France* which described his journeys prior to the revolution. Young was the son of a chaplain and became a farmer at the age of twenty-two. He was an agriculturalist writing a number of books on the topic. He travelled throughout England, Ireland and later France, his writings documenting his journeys. Though he focused primarily on the land and agriculture, he also touched on the situation in France and the events leading up to the revolution in 1789. The later essay, *The Example of France,* showed a shift in his position regarding the uprising. His account of the problem arising out of revolution put him in agreement with none other than Edmund Burke.

Young shifted his position away from earlier support of the revolution when the government began doing something he found horrifying – confiscating property from farmers. He stated "I have been too long a farmer to be governed by anything but events" (Young). His essay was meant to warn his fellow farmers of what could happen:

> Let the farmers of this kingdom represent
> to themselves a picture of what their
> situation would be, if their labourers, their

servants, and the paupers whom they
support by poors-rates, were all armed,
and, in some measure, regimented, and
in possession of the vestry, voting not
only the money to be raised by rates, but
the division of it among themselves;
decreeing what the price of the farmer's
products should be; what wages should
be paid to servants, and what pay to
labourers. Under such a system of
government I beg to ask, what security
would remain for a single shilling in the
pockets of those who are at present in a
state of ease and affluence? (Young)

His farming background clearly influenced his opinion
and he summed it up in the close of his essay:

The quarrel now raging in that once
flourishing kingdom, is not between
liberty and tyranny, or between
protecting and oppressive systems of
government; it is, on the contrary
collected to a single point, – it is alone a
question of property; it is a trial at arms,
whether those who have *nothing* shall

> not seize and possess the property of
> those who have *something*. (Young)

While, like Burke, Young no longer supported the revolution, his reasons were far different. Young's position as a farmer and landowner caused him to fear a similar uprising in England whereas Burke's interest was in protecting the status quo of the monarchy. Background rather than their years colored the opinions of Price, Burke, Paine and Young. Though ranging in age from fifty-two to sixty-six the men could be thought of as contemporaries belonging to an older generation.

Somewhat younger at the time of the revolution, William Godwin, like Price, was the son of a strict Calvinist minister and, again like Price, a Dissenting minister himself. Unlike the wealthy background of Price and Burke, he had a middle-class upbringing. In 1793, at the age of thirty-seven, Godwin published the book *Enquiry Concerning Political Justice and its Influence on Morals and Happiness,* a relatively lengthy volume. Rather than directly supporting the French revolution, Godwin's work is more theoretical in nature though there is clearly a connection.

Godwin makes a general statement about revolution when he states "Revolution is engendered by an indignation against tyranny" (Godwin). He also says that "government, even in its best state, is an evil" (Godwin). He does appear to have more radical views than the previous writers who were favorably inclined toward the French revolution. One of the chapters in his book is titled "Of the dissolution of Government." In it he writes:

> With what delight must every well informed friend of mankind look forward, to the auspicious period, the dissolution of political government, of that brute engine, which has been the only perennial cause of the vices of mankind, and which, as has abundantly appeared in the progress of the present work, has mischiefs of various sorts incorporated with its substances, and no otherwise removable than by its utter annihilation! (Godwin)

Godwin seems to be blaming government for everything that is wrong with man. Price and Paine were more against the tyranny of the French monarchy than the government itself. Young, too, was originally in support of the revolt because he personally witnessed the struggle of the French population, he changed his view only after the new government started confiscating the property and wealth of farmers. None of those men were nearly as extreme as to want the "utter annihilation" of government such as Godwin proposed. His writing suggest that more than just a revolution, he was supporting anarchy.

A year and a half younger than Godwin, William Blake expressed his views on the revolution in a much more succinct manner. Blake, a printer by trade, was a painter and poet. Around the time of Paine's *Rights of man*, but before Godwin's and Young's publications, Blake wrote the poem *The French Revolution: a Poem in Seven Books*. The title indicated a longer work but only the first book was ever known to be written. The poem shows Blake's sympathy for the revolt with the images he employs and reads like an historical account as he tells of the events unfolding at the beginning of the revolution, the fall of the Bastille and the time that immediately follows.

The poem begins with a somber mood, "The Dead brood" (1) and the feeling of turmoil, "France shakes" (16) as the revolution begins, "the Bastille trembles" (18). Inmates of the prison are described including one driven mad as "he was confin'd / For a letter of advice to a King" (50-51), an indication that he was a political prisoner. Later in the poem Blake takes a celebratory tone, "'Hear, O heavens of France! the voice of the people, arising from valley and hill," (205). Near the end Blake shows the King's defeat, "Pale and cold sat the King in midst of his Peers, and his noble heart sunk" (294) and ended with the phrase, "Senate in peace sat beneath morning's beam" (306) indicating power had shifted and peace, and by implication prosperity, would now exist for the people of France. The previous essayists works did not require the interpretation a poem such as Blake's required. Despite this his position favoring the revolt is quite clear.

The first response to Burke's essay came not from Blake's 1791 poem or Paine's essay that same year but from a young woman whose ire Burke's essay raised. Mary Wollstonecraft was the eldest daughter of a wealthy, but heavy drinking and physically abusive, man. She left home at the age of nineteen seeking to earn her own way. In 1784 she, along with her sister and a friend, established a school. Though the school eventually failed, her experience inspired her to write *THOUGHTS ON THE EDUCATION OF DAUGHTERS* in 1787. After a failed marriage she would go on to wed another essayist, William Godwin, in1797 though she would die later that year shortly after giving birth to their daughter. Later known for her feminist writing, Mary Wollstonecraft was just thirty-one years of age when she responded to Burke's essay by writing *A Vindication of the Rights of Men* in 1790.

Reflections on the Revolution in France was so offensive to Wollstonecraft that, unlike the other essayists represented, she didn't respond by making an eloquent case for her own position, she engaged in a direct attack on Burke's points, often in an ad hominem manner. Her essay was structured as a letter to Burke which was preceded by an advertisement in which she stated, "my indignation was roused by the sophistical arguments, that every moment crossed me" and in the beginning of the letter she says "I should believe you to be a good, though a vain man, if some circumstances in your conduct did not render the inflexibility of your integrity doubtful" (Wollstonecraft).

Wollstonecraft believed that Burke often contradicted his own arguments and she stated, "I glow with indignation when I attempt, methodically, to unravel your slavish paradoxes, in which I can find no fixed first principle to refute" and "you affirm in one page what you deny in another; and how frequently you draw conclusions without any previous premises." Toward the end of her letter she wrote, "I find it almost impossible candidly to refute your sophisms, without quoting your own words, and putting the numerous contradictions I observed in opposition to each other." She continued to add personal assaults on his character saying such things as, "I perceive, from the whole tenor of your Reflections, that you have a mortal antipathy to reason" (Wollstonecraft).

In a later portion of the letter she describes her position on the concept of an inherited monarchy:

> The civilization which has taken place in
> Europe has been very partial, and, like
> every custom that an arbitrary point of
> honour has established, refines the
> manners at the expence of morals, by
> making sentiments and opinions current
> in conversation that have no root in the

heart, or weight in the cooler resolves of
the mind.–And what has stopped its
progress?– hereditary property–
hereditary honours. The man has been
changed into an artificial monster by the
station in which he was born.
(Wollstonecraft)

While Burke views the monarchy as a tradition "from a
long line of ancestors," she refers to it as "the venerable
vestiges of ancient days" (Wollstonecraft). While
Wollstonecraft scoffs at the notion of gaining a title solely as an
accident of birth, she strongly states that there are basic
human rights everyone receives regardless of the social class:

It is necessary emphatically to repeat,
that there are rights which men inherit
at their birth, as rational creatures, who
were raised above the brute creation by
their improvable faculties; and that, in
receiving these, not from their
forefathers but, from God, prescription
can never undermine natural rights.
(Wollstonecraft)

These rights are echoed later by the sentiments expressed
by Thomas Paine in his essay *The Rights of Man* in 1791.

Wollstonecraft found Burke's attitude toward the poor especially distasteful, "your contempt for the poor always appears conspicuous, and rouses my indignation" she continues "They have a right to more comfort than they at present enjoy; and more comfort might be afforded them, without encroaching on the pleasures of the rich" (Wollstonecraft). Economic disparity between the French aristocracy and the citizenry was a primary driver of the French revolution. Burke defends this disparity which Wollstonecraft despises.

Wollstonecraft was not the only woman to weigh in on the French Revolution. Helen Maria Williams was born in London three years after Wollstonecraft. Her father, an army officer, died when Williams was eight after which her family moved to northern England. She returned to London and, at the age of twenty-two, wrote a poem which spoke of the effects Spanish colonialism had on the native people of Peru. She was the inspiration for a poem by William Wordsworth, *Sonnet on seeing Miss Helen Maria Williams Weep at a Tale of Distress,* written in 1787. In London she was known to associate with radical thinkers including William Godwin. In 1790 she travelled alone, against the norms of the time, to revolutionary France.

In *Letters Written in France* Williams provides a first-hand account of events occurring during the revolution. In her opening letter she says "had I not reached Paris at the moment I did reach it, I should have missed the most sublime spectacle which, perhaps, was ever represented on the theatre of this earth" (Williams). She was referring to the "Fête de la Federation" which was a celebration held July 14th, 1790 commemorating the one-year anniversary of the fall of the Bastille.

      The tone of her letter was upbeat as she delighted in the event she witnessed:

> I Promised to send you a description of the Federation; but it is not to be described! One must have been present, to form any judgment of a scene, the sublimity of which depended much less on its external magnificence than on the effect it produced on the minds of the spectators.... Half a million of people assembled at a spectacle, which furnished every image that can elevate the mind of man; which connected the enthusiasm of moral sentiment with the solemn pomp of religious ceremonies; which addressed itself at once to the imagination, the understanding, and the heart! (Williams)

She delighted in the occasion since she supported the revolution and she said, "You will not suspect that I was an indifferent witness of such a scene" (Williams). Though Williams was English, her sentiments made it seems as if she had taken part in the revolution herself and was now victorious:

> It was the triumph of human kind; it was man asserting the noblest privilege of his nature; and it required but the common feelings of humanity, to become in that moment a citizen of the world. For myself, I acknowledge that my heart caught with enthusiasm the general sympathy; my eyes were filled with tears; and I shall never forget the sensations of that day, 'while memory holds her seat in my bosom.' (Williams)

In another letter she described her visit to the Bastille prison of which she said, "After having visited the Bastille, we may indeed by surprised, that a nation so enlightened as the French, submitted so long to the oppressions of their government" (Williams). She later described her journey through the streets of Paris and her final letter depicts her leaving France and returning to England.

Williams went back to France the following year. Though she was imprisoned for a time for being British and expressed disdain for much of what happened during the Reign of Terror under Robespierre, she never lost her love of

France. She went to Switzerland for a short time to avoid persecution but returned to France and lived there for the remainder of her life.

From the descriptions of the essayists and how they responded to each it is possible to see the differing political opinions of their time. Even those in agreement varied in the extremes to which they supported or opposed the French Revolution, much as political bloggers of the current century vary from those calmly relating well-reasoned positions to those spewing pure venom.

Despite the stereotype of youthful idealism the age of the writer did not seem to be a major factor in their position. What did matter was the sex and, even more so, the economic and social background of the essayist. Though most clearly illustrated in the position of Young, the farmer, the personal life journey seemed to play the largest role in informing the writer's respective opinions.

The Elder Statesmen

Richard Price (1723-1791)

A Discourse on the Love of Our Country

(1789)

Edmund Burke (1729-1797)

Reflections on the Revolution in France

(1790)

A Discourse on the Love of Our Country

Richard Price (1723-1791)

PsalmCxxii. 2d, And Following Verses.

*Our feet shall stand within thy gates, O Jerusalem,
whither the tribes go up; the tribes of the Lord unto the
testimony of Israel. To give thanks to the name of the Lord, for
there sit the thrones of judgment; the throne of the House of
David. Pray for the peace of Jerusalem. They shall prosper
that love thee. Peace be within thy walls, and prosperity within
thy palaces. For my brethren and companions sake I will now
say peace be within thee. Because of the House of the Lord
our God, I will seek thy good.*

IN these words the Psalmist expresses, in strong and
beautiful language, his love of his country, and the reasons on
which he founded it; and my present design is, to take
occasion from them to explain the duty we owe to our country,
and the nature, foundation, and proper expressions of that love
to it which we ought to cultivate.

I reckon this a subject particularly suitable to the
services of this day, and to the Anniversary of our deliverance
at the Revolution from the dangers of popery and arbitrary
power; and should I, on such an occasion, be led to touch
more on political subjects than would at any other time be
proper in the pulpit, you will, I doubt not, excuse me.

The love of our country has in all times been a subject
of warm commendations; and it is certainly a noble passion;
but, like all other passions, it requires regulation and direction.
There are mistakes and prejudices by which, in this instance,
we are in particular danger of being misled.—I will briefly
mention some of these to you, and observe,

First, That by our country is meant, in this case, not
the soil or the spot of earth on which we happen to have been
born; not the forests and fields, but that community of which
we are members; or that body of companions and friends and
kindred who are associated with us under the same
constitution of government, protected by the same laws, and
bound together by the same civil polity.

Secondly, It is proper to observe, that even in this sense of our country, that love of it which is our duty, does not imply any conviction of the superior value of it to other countries, or any particular preference of its laws and constitution of government. Were this implied, the love of their country would be the duty of only a very small part of mankind; for there are few countries that enjoy the advantage of laws and governments which deserve to be preferred. To found, therefore, this duty on such a preference, would be to found it on error and delusion. It is, however, a common delusion. There is the same partiality in countries, to themselves, that there is in individuals. All our attachments should be accompanied, as far as possible, with right opinions.—We are too apt to confine wisdom and virtue within the circle of our own acquaintance and party. Our friends, our country, and in short everything related to us, we are disposed to overvalue. A wise man will guard himself against this delusion. He will study to think of all things as they are, and not suffer any partial affections to blind his understanding. In other families there may be as much worth as in our own. In other circles of friends there may be as much wisdom; and in other countries as much of all that deserves esteem; but, notwithstanding this our obligation to love our own families, friends, and country, and to seek, in the first place, their good, will remain the same.

Thirdly, It is proper I should desire you particularly to distinguish between the love of our country and that spirit of rivalship and ambition which has been common among nations.—What has the love of their country hitherto been among mankind? What has it been but a love of domination; a desire of conquest, and a thirst for grandeur and glory, by extending territory, and enslaving surrounding countries? What has it been but a blind and narrow principle, producing in every country a contempt of other countries, and forming men into combinations and factions against their common rights and liberties? This is the principle that has been too often cried up as a virtue of the first rank: a principle of the same kind with that which governs clans of Indians or tribes of Arabs, and leads them out to plunder and massacre. As most of the evils which have taken place in private life, and among individuals, have been occasioned by the desire of private interest overcoming the public affections; so most of the evils which have taken place among bodies of men have been occasioned by the desire of their own interest overcoming the principle of universal benevolence: and leading them to attack one another's territories, to encroach on one another's rights, and to endeavour to build their own advancement on the degradation of all within the reach of their power—What was the love of their country among the Jews, but a wretched partiality to themselves, and a proud contempt of all other nations? What was the love of their country among the old Romans? We have heard much of it; but I cannot hesitate in saying that, however great it appeared in some of its exertions, it was in general no better than a principle holding together a band of robbers in their attempts to crush all liberty but their own. What is now the love of his country in a Spaniard, a Turk, or a Russian? Can it be considered as anything better than a passion for slavery, or a blind attachment to a spot where he enjoys no rights, and is disposed of as if he was a beast?

Let us learn by such reflexions to correct and purify this passion, and to make it a just and rational principle of action.

It is very remarkable that the founder of our religion has not once mentioned this duty, or given us any recommendation of it; and this has, by unbelievers, been made an objection to Christianity. What I have said will entirely remove this objection. Certain it is, that, by inculcating on men an attachment to their country, Christianity would, at the time it was propagated, have done unspeakably more harm than good. Among the Jews, it would have been an excitement to war and insurrections; for they were then in eager expectation of becoming soon (as the favourite people of Heaven) the lords and conquerors of the earth, under the triumphant reign of the Messiah. Among the Romans, likewise, this principle had, as I have just observed, exceeded its just bounds, and rendered them enemies to the peace and happiness of mankind. By inculcating it, therefore, Christianity would have confirmed both Jews and Gentiles in one of the most pernicious faults. Our Lord and his Apostles have done better. They have recommended that universal benevolence which is an unspeakably nobler principle than any partial affections. They have laid such stress on loving all men, even our enemies, and made an ardent and extensive charity so essential a part of virtue, that the religion they have preached may, by way of distinction from all other religions, be called the Religion of Benevolence. Nothing can be more friendly to the general rights of mankind; and were it duly regarded and practised, every man would consider every other man as his brother, and all the animosity that now takes place among contending nations would be abolished. If you want any proof of this, think of our Saviour's parable of the good Samaritan. The Jews and Samaritans were two rival nations that entertained a hatred of one another the most inveterate. The design of this parable was to shew to a Jew, that even a Samaritan,and consequently all men of all nations and religions, were included in the precept, Thou shalt love thy neighbour as thyself.

But I am digressing from what I had chiefly in view; which was, after noticing that love of our country which is false and spurious, to explain the nature and effects of that which is just and reasonable. With this view I must desire you to recollect that we are so constituted that our affections are more drawn to some among mankind than to others, in proportion to their degrees of nearness to us, and our power of being useful to them. It is obvious that this is a circumstance in the constitution of our natures which proves the wisdom and goodness of our Maker; for had our affections been determined alike to all our fellow-creatures, human life would have been a scene of embarrassment and distraction. Our regards, according to the order of nature, begin with ourselves; and every man is charged primarily with the care of himself. Next come our families, and benefactors, and friends; and after them our country. We can do little for the interest of mankind at large. To this interest, however, all other interests are subordinate. The noblest principle in our nature is the regard to general justice, and that good-will which embraces all the world.—I have already observed this; but it cannot be too often repeated. Though our immediate attention must be employed in promoting our own interest and that of our nearest connexions; yet we must remember, that a narrower interest ought always to give way to a more extensive interest. In pursuing particularly the interest of our country, we ought to carry our views beyond it. We should love it ardently, but not exclusively. We ought to seek its good, by all the means that our different circumstances and abilities will allow; but at the same time we ought to consider ourselves as citizens of the world, and take care to maintain a just regard to the rights of other countries.

The enquiry by what means (subject to this limitation) we may best promote the interest of our country is very important; and all that remains of this discourse shall be employed in answering it, and in exhorting you to manifest your love to your country, by the means I shall mention.

The chief blessings of human nature are the three following:—Truth—Virtue—and Liberty.—These are, therefore, the blessings in the possession of which the interest of our country lies, and to the attainment of which our love of it ought to direct our endeavours. By the diffusion of knowledge it must be distinguished from a country of Barbarians: by the practice of religious virtue, it must be distinguished from a country o gamblers, Atheists, and libertines: and by the possession of liberty, it must be distinguished from a country of slaves.—I will dwell for a few moments on each of these heads:

Our first concern, as lovers of our country, must be to enlighten it.—Why are the nations of the world so patient under despotism?—Why do they crouch to tyrants, and submit to be treated as if they were a herd of cattle? Is it not because they are kept in darkness, and want knowledge? Enlighten them and you will elevate them. Shew them they are men, and they will act like men. Give them just ideas of civil government, and let them know that it is an expedient for gaining protection against injury and defending their rights*, and it will be impossible for them to submit to governments which, like most of those now in the world, are usurpations on the rights of men, and little better than contrivances for enabling the few to oppress the many. Convince them that the Deity is a righteous and benevolent as well as omnipotent being, who regards with equal eye all his creatures, and connects his favour with nothing but an honest desire to know and do his will; and that zeal for mystical doctrines which has led men to hate and harass one another will be exterminated. Set religion before them as a rational service, consisting not in any rites and ceremonies, but in worshipping God with a pure heart and practising righteousness from the fear of his displeasure and the apprehension of a future righteous judgment, and that gloomy and cruel superstition will be abolished which has hitherto gone under the name of religion, and to the support of which civil government has been perverted.—Ignorance is the parent of bigotry, intolerance, persecution and slavery. Inform and instruct mankind; and these evils will be excluded.— Happy is the person who, himself raised above vulgar errors, is conscious of having aimed at giving mankind this instruction. Happy is the Scholar or Philosopher who at the close of life can reflect that he has made this use of his learning and abilities: but happier far must he be, if at the same time he has reason to believe he has been successful, and actually contributed, by his instructions, to disseminate among his fellow-creatures just notions of themselves, of their rights, of religion, and the nature and end of civil government. Such were Milton, Locke, Sidney, Hoadly, in this country; such were Montesquieu, Fenelon, Turgot, in France. They sowed a seed which has since taken root, and is now growing up to a glorious harvest. To the information they conveyed by their writings we owe those revolutions in which every friend to mankind is now exulting.—What an encouragement is this to us all in our endeavours to enlighten the world? Every degree of illumination which we can communicate must do the greatest good. It helps to prepare the minds of men for the recovery of their rights, and hastens the overthrow of priest craft and tyranny.—In short, we may, in this instance, learn our duty from the conduct of the oppressors of the world. They know that light is hostile to them, and therefore they labour to keep men in the dark. With this intention they have appointed licensers of the press; and, in Popish countries, prohibited the reading of the Bible. Remove the darkness in which they envelope the world, and their usurpations will be exposed, their power will be subverted, and the world emancipated.

The next great blessing of human nature which I have mentioned is virtue. This ought to follow knowledge, and to be directed by it. Virtue without knowledge makes enthusiasts; and knowledge without virtue makes devils; but both united elevates to the top of human dignity and perfection.—We must, therefore, if we would serve our country, make both these the objects of our zeal. We must discourage vice in all its forms; and our endeavours to enlighten must have ultimately in view a reformation of manners and virtuous practice.

I must add here, that in the practice of virtue I include the discharge of the public duties of religion. By neglecting these we may injure our country essentially. But it is melancholy to observe that it is a common neglect among us; and in a great measure owing to a cause which is not likely to be soon removed: I mean, the defects (may I not say, the absurdities?) in our established codes of faith and worship. In foreign countries, the higher ranks of men, not distinguishing between the religion they see established and the Christian religion, are generally driven to irreligion and infidelity. The like evil is produced by the like cause in this country; and if no reformation of our established formularies can be brought about, it must be expected that religion will go on to lose its credit, and that little of it will be left except among the lower orders of people, many of whom, while their superiors give up all religion, are sinking into a barbarism in religion lately revived by Methodism, and mistaking, as the world has generally done, the service acceptable to God for a system of faith souring the temper, and a service of forms supplanting morality.

I hope you will not mistake what I am now saying, or consider it as the effect of my prejudices as a Dissenter from the established church. The complaint I am making, is the complaint of many of the wisest and best men in the established church itself, who have been long urging the necessity of a revisal of its Liturgy and Articles*. These were framed above two centuries ago, when Christendom was just emerging from the ignorance and barbarity of the dark ages. They remain now much the same they were then; and, therefore, cannot be properly adapted to the good sense and liberality of the present times.—This imperfection, however, in our public forms of worship, affords no excuse to any person for neglecting public worship. All communities will have some religion; and it is of infinite consequence that they should be led to that which, by enforcing the obligations of virtue and putting men upon loving instead of damning one another, is most favourable to the interest of society.

If there is a Governor of the world, who directs all events, he ought to be invoked and worshipped; and those who dislike that mode of worship which is prescribed by public authority, ought (if they can find no worship out of the church which they approve) to set up a separate worship for themselves; and by doing this, and giving an example of a rational and manly worship, men of weight, from their rank or literature, may do the greatest service to society and the world. They may bear a testimony against that application of civil power to the support of particular modes of faith, which obstructs human improvement, and perpetuates error; and they may hold out an instruction which will discountenance superstition, and at the same time recommend religion, by making it appear to be (what it certainly is when rightly understood) the strongest incentive to all that is generous and worthy, and consequently the best friend to public order and happiness.

Liberty is the next great blessing which I have mentioned as the object of patriotic zeal. It is inseparable from knowledge and virtue, and together with them completes the glory of a community. An enlightened and virtuous country must be a free country. It cannot suffer invasions of its rights, or bend to tyrants.—I need not, on this occasion, take any pains to shew you how great a blessing liberty is. The smallest attention to the history of past ages, and the present state of mankind, will make you sensible of its importance. Look round the world, and you will find almost every country, respectable or contemptible, happy or miserable, a fruitful field or a frightful waste, according as it possesses or wants this blessing. Think of Greece, formerly the seat of arts and science, and the most distinguished spot under heaven; but now, having lost liberty, a vile and wretched spot, a region of darkness, poverty, and barbarity.—Such reflexions must convince you that, if you love your country, you cannot be zealous enough in promoting the cause of liberty in it. But it will come in my way to say more to this purpose presently.

The observations I have made include our whole duty to our country; for by endeavouring to liberalize and enlighten it, to discourage vice and to promote virtue in it, and to assert and support its liberties, we shall endeavour to do all that is necessary to make it great and happy.—But it is proper that, on this occasion, I should be more explicit, and exemplify our duty to our country by observing farther, that it requires us to obey its laws, and to respect its magistrates.

Civil government (as I have before observed) is an institution of human prudence for guarding our persons, our property, and our good name, against invasion; and for securing to the members of a community that liberty to which all have an equal right, as far as they do not, by any overt act, use it to injure the liberty of others. Civil laws are regulations agreed upon by the community for gaining these ends*; and civil magistrates are officers appointed by the community for executing these laws. Obedience, therefore, to the laws and to magistrates, are necessary expressions of our regard to the community; and without this obedience the ends of government cannot be obtained, or a community avoid falling into a state of anarchy that will destroy those rights and subvert that liberty, which government is instituted to protect.

I wish it was in my power to give you a just account of the importance of this observation. It shews the ground on which the duty of obeying civil governors stands, and that there are two extremes in this case which ought to be avoided.—These extremes are adulation and servility on one hand; and a and licentious contempt on the other. The former is the extreme to which mankind in general have been most prone; for it has oftener happened that men have been too passive than too unruly; and the rebellion of Kings against their people has been more common, and done more mischief, than the rebellion of people against their Kings.

Adulation is always odious, and when offered to men in power it corrupts them, by giving them improper ideas of their situation; and it debases those who offer it, by manifesting an abjectness founded on improper ideas of themselves. I have lately observed in this kingdom too near approaches to this abjectness. In our late addresses to the King, on his recovery from the severe illness with which God has been pleased to afflict him, we have appeared more like a herd crawling at the feet of a master, than like enlightened and manly citizens rejoicing with a beloved sovereign, but at the same time conscious that he derives all his consequence from themselves. But, perhaps, these servilities in the language of our late addresses should be pardoned, as only forms of civility and expressions of an overflow of good-nature. They have, however, a dangerous tendency. The potentates of this world are sufficiently apt to consider themselves as possessed of an inherent superiority, which gives them a right to govern, and makes mankind their own; and this infatuation is almost everywhere fostered in them by the creeping sycophants about them, and the language of flattery which they are continually hearing.

Civil governors are properly the servants of the public; and a King is no more than the first servant of the public, created by it, maintained by it, and responsible to it: and all the homage paid him, is due to him on no other account than his relation to the public. His sacredness is the sacredness of the community. His authority is the authority of the community; and the term Majesty, which it is usual to apply to him, is by no means his own majesty, but the majesty of the people. For this reason, whatever he may be in his private capacity; and though, in respect of personal qualities, not equal to, or even far below many among ourselves—For this reason, I say, (that is, as representing the community and its first magistrate), he is entitled to our reverence and obedience. The words most excellent majesty are rightly applied to him; and there is a respect which it would be criminal to withhold from him.

You cannot be too attentive to this observation. The improvement of the world depends on the attention to it: nor will mankind be ever as virtuous and happy as they are capable of being, till the attention to it becomes universal and efficacious. If we forget it, we shall be in danger of an idolatry as gross and stupid as that of the ancient heathens, who, after fabricating blocks of wood or stone, fell down and worshipped them.—The disposition in mankind to this kind of idolatry is indeed a very mortifying subject of reflexion.—In Turkey, millions of human beings adore a silly mortal, and are ready to throw themselves at his feet, and to submit their lives to his discretion.—In Russia, the common people are only a stock on the lands of grandees, or appendages to their estates, which, like the fixtures in a house, are bought and sold with the estates. In Spain, in Germany, and under most of the governments of the world, mankind are in a similar state of humiliation. Who, that has a just sense of the dignity of his nature, can avoid execrating such a debasement of it?

Had I been to address the King on a late occasion, I should have been inclined to do it in a style very different from that of most of the addressers, and to use some such language as the following:—"I rejoice, Sir, in your recovery. I thank God for his goodness to you. I honour you not only as my King, but as almost the only lawful King in the world, because the only one who owes his crown to the choice of his people. May you enjoy all possible happiness. May God shew you the folly of those effusions of adulation which you are now receiving, and guard you against their effects. May you be led to such a just sense of the nature of your situation, and endowed with such wisdom, as shall render your restoration to the government of these kingdoms a blessing to it, and engage you to consider yourself as more properly the Servant than the Sovereign of your people."

But I must not forget the opposite extreme to that now taken notice of; that is, a disdainful pride, derived from a consciousness of equality, or, perhaps, superiority, in respect of all that gives true dignity to men in power, and producing a contempt of them, and a disposition to treat them with rudeness and insult. It is a trite observation, that extremes generally beget one another. This is particularly true in the present case. Persons justly informed on the subject of government, when they see men dazzled by looking up to high stations, and observe loyalty carried to a length that implies ignorance and servility: such persons, in such circumstances, are in danger of spurning at all public authority, and throwing off that respectful demeanor to persons invested with it which the order of society requires. There is undoubtedly a particular deference and homage due to civil magistrates, on account of their stations and offices; nor can that man be either truly wise or truly virtuous, who despises governments, and wantonly speaks evil of his rulers; or who does not, by all the means in his power, endeavour to strengthen their hands, and to give weight to their exertions in the discharge of their duty.—Fear God, says St. Peter. Love the brotherhood. Honour all men. Honour the King.—You must needs, says St. Paul, be subject to rulers, not only for wrath(that is, from the fear of suffering the penalties annexed to the breach of the laws),but for conscience sake. For rulers are ministers of God, and revengers for executing wrath on all that do evil.

Another expression of our love to our country is defending it against enemies. These enemies are of two sorts, internal and external; or domestic and foreign. The former are the most dangerous, and they have generally been the most successful. I have just observed, that there is a submission due to the executive officers of government, which is our duty; but you must not forget what I have also observed, that it must not be a blind and slavish submission. Men in power (unless better disposed than is common) are always endeavouring to extend their power. They hate the doctrine, that it is a trust derived from the people, and not a right vested in themselves. For this reason, the tendency of every government is to despotism; and in this the best constituted governments must end, if the people are not vigilant, ready to take alarms, and determined to resist abuses as soon as they begin. This vigilance, therefore, it is our duty to maintain. Whenever it is withdrawn, and a people cease to reason about their rights and to be awake to encroachments, they are in danger of being enslaved, and their servants will soon become their masters.

I need not say how much it is our duty to defend our country against foreign enemies. When a country is attacked in any of its rights by another country, or when any attempts are made by ambitious foreign powers to injure it, a war in its defence becomes necessary: and, in such circumstances, to die for our country is meritorious and noble. These defensive wars are, in my opinion, the only just wars. Offensive wars are always unlawful; and to seek the aggrandizement of our country by them, that is, by attacking other countries, in order to extend dominion, or to gratify avarice, is wicked and detestable. Such, however, have been most of the wars which have taken place in the world; but the time is, I hope, coming, when a conviction will prevail, of the folly*as well as the iniquity of wars; and when the nations of the earth, happy under just governments, and no longer in danger from the passions of Kings, will find out better ways of settling their disputes; and beat (as Isaiah prophecies) their swords into plowshares, and their spears into pruning-hooks.

Among the particulars included in that duty to our country, by discharging which we should shew our love to it, I will only further mention praying for it, and offering up thanksgivings to God for every event favourable to it. At the present season we are called upon to express, in this way, our love to our country. It is the business of this day, and of the present service; and, therefore, it is necessary that I should now direct your attention to it particularly.

We are met to thank God for that event in this country to which the name of The Revolution has been given; and which, for more than a century, it has been usual for the friends of freedom, and more especially Protestant Dissenters, under the title of theRevolution Society,to celebrate with expressions of joy and exultation.—My highly valued and excellent friend*, who addressed you on this occasion last year, has given you an interesting account of the principal circumstances that attended this event, and of the reasons we have for rejoicing in it. By a bloodless victory, the fetters which despotism had been long preparing for us were broken; the rights of the people were asserted, a tyrant expelled, and a Sovereign of our own choice appointed in his room. Security was given to our property, and our consciences were emancipated. The bounds of free enquiry were enlarged; the volume in which are the words of eternal life, was laid more open to our examination; and that era of light and liberty was introduced among us, by which we have been made an example to other kingdoms, and became the instructors of the world. Had it not been for this deliverance, the probability is, that, instead of being thus distinguished, we should now have been a base people, groaning under the infamy and misery of popery and slavery. Let us, therefore, offer thanksgivings to God, the author of all our blessings. Had he not been on our side, we should have been swallowed up quick, and the proud waters would have gone over our souls. But our souls are escaped, and the snare has been broken. Blessed then be the name of the Lord, who made heaven and earth. cxxivth Psalm.

It is well known that King James was not far from gaining his purpose; and that probably he would have succeeded, had he been less in a hurry. But he was a fool as well as a bigot. He wanted courage as well as prudence; and, therefore, fled, and left us to settle quietly for ourselves that constitution of government which is now our boast. We have particular reason, as Protestant Dissenters, to rejoice on this occasion. It was at this time we were rescued from persecution, and obtained the liberty of worshipping God in the manner we think most acceptable to him. It was then our meeting-houses were opened, our worship was taken under the protection of the law, and the principles of toleration gained a triumph. We have, therefore, on this occasion, peculiar reasons for thanksgiving—But let us remember that we ought not to satisfy ourselves with thanksgivings. Our gratitude, if genuine, will be accompanied with endeavours to give stability to the deliverance our country has obtained, and to extend and improve the happiness with which the Revolution has blest us—Let us, in particular, take care not to forget the principles of the Revolution. This Society has, very properly, in its Reports, held out these principles, as an instruction to the public. I will only take notice of the three following:

First; The right to liberty of conscience in religious matters.

Secondly; The right to resist power when abused. And,

Thirdly; The right to chuse our own governors; to cashier them for misconduct; and to frame a government for ourselves.

On these three principles, and more especially the last, was the Revolution founded. Were it not true that liberty of conscience is a sacred right; that power abused justifies resistance; and that civil authority is a delegation from the people—Were not, I say, all this true; the Revolution would have been not an assertion, but an invasion of rights; not a Revolution, but a Rebellion. Cherish in your breasts this conviction, and act under its influence; detesting the odious doctrines of passive obedience, nonresistance, and the divine right of kings—doctrines which, had they been acted upon in this country, would have left us at this time wretched slaves—doctrines which imply, that God made mankind to be oppressed and plundered; and which are no less a blasphemy against him, than an insult on common sense.

I would farther direct you to remember, that though the Revolution was a great work, it was by no means a perfect work; and that all was not then gained which was necessary to put the kingdom in the secure and complete possession of the blessings of liberty.—In particular, you should recollect, that the toleration then obtained was imperfect. It included only those who could declare their faith in the doctrinal articles of the church of England. It has, indeed, been since extended, but not sufficiently; for there still exist penal laws on account of religious opinions, which (were they carried into execution) would shut up many of our places of worship, and silence and imprison some of our ablest and best men.—The test laws are also still in force; and deprive of eligibility to civil and military offices, all who cannot conform to the established worship. It is with great pleasure I find that the body of Protestant Dissenters, though defeated in two late attempts to deliver their country from this disgrace to it, have determined to persevere. Should they at last succeed, they will have the satisfaction, not only of removing from themselves a proscription they do not deserve, but of contributing to lessen the number of our public iniquities. For I cannot call by a gentler name, laws which convert an ordinance appointed by our Saviour to commemorate his death, into an instrument of oppressive policy, and a qualification of rakes and atheists for civil posts.—I have said, should they succeed—but perhaps I ought not to suggest a doubt about their success*. And, indeed, when I consider that in Scotland the established church is defended by no such test—that in Ireland it has been abolished—that in a great neighbouring country it has been declared to be an indefeasible right of all citizens to be equally eligible to public offices—that in the same kingdom a professed Dissenter from the established church holds the first office in the state—that in the Emperor's dominions Jews have been lately admitted to the enjoyment of equal privileges with other citizens—and that in this very country, a Dissenter, though excluded from the power of executing the laws, yet is allowed to be employed in making them.—When, I say, I consider such facts as these, I am disposed to think it impossible that the enemies of the repeal of the Test Laws should not soon become ashamed, and give up their opposition.

But the most important instance of the imperfect state in which the Revolution left our constitution, is the inequality of our representation.I think, indeed, this defect in our constitution so gross and so palpable, as to make it excellent chiefly in form and theory. You should remember that a representation in the legislature of a kingdom is the basis of constitutional liberty in it, and of all legitimate government; and that without it a government is nothing but an usurpation*. When the representation is fair and equal, and at the same time vested with such powers as our House of Commons possesses, a kingdom may be said to govern itself, and consequently to possess true liberty. When the representation is partial, a kingdom possesses liberty only partially; and if extremely partial, it only gives a semblance of liberty; but if not only extremely partial, but corruptly chosen, and under corrupt influence after being chosen, it becomes anuisance,and produces the worst of all forms of government—a government by corruption—a government carried on and supported by spreading venality and profligacy through a kingdom. May heaven preserve this kingdom from a calamity so dreadful! It is the point of depravity to which abuses under such a government as ours naturally tend, and the last stage of national unhappiness. We are, at present, I hope, at a great distance from it. But it cannot be pretended that there are no advances towards it, or that there is no reason for apprehension and alarm.

The inadequateness of our representation has been long a subject of complaint. This is, in truth, our fundamental grievance; and I do not think that anything is much more our duty, as men who love their country, and are grateful for the Revolution, than to unite our zeal in endeavouring to get it redressed. At the time of the American war, associations were formed for this purpose in London, and other parts of the kingdom; and our present Minister himself has, since that war, directed to it an effort which made him a favourite with many of us. But all attention to it seems now lost, and the probability is, that this inattention will continue, and that nothing will be done towards gaining for us this essential blessing, till some great calamity again alarms our fears, or till some great abuse of power again provokes our resentment; or, perhaps, till the acquisition of a pure and equal representation by other countries (while we are mocked with the shadow*) kindles our shame.

Such is the conduct by which we ought to express our gratitude for the Revolution.—We should always bear in mind the principles that justify it. We should contribute all we can towards supplying what it left deficient; and shew ourselves anxious about transmitting the blessings obtained by it to our posterity, unimpaired and improved.—But, brethren, while we thus shew our patriotic zeal, let us take care not to disgrace the cause of patriotism, by any licentious, or immoral conduct.—Oh! how earnestly do I wish that all who profess zeal in this cause, were as distinguished by the purity of their morals, as some of them are by their abilities; and that I could make them sensible of the advantages they would derive from a virtuous character, and of the suspicions they incur and the loss of consequence they suffer by wanting it.—Oh! that I could see in men who oppose tyranny in the state, a disdain of the tyranny of low passions in themselves; or, at least, such a sense of shame, and regard to public order and decency as would induce them to hide their irregularities, and to avoid insulting the virtuous part of the community by an open exhibition of vice!—I cannot reconcile myself to the idea of an immoral patriot, or to that separation of private from public virtue, which some think to be possible. Is it to be expected that— But I must forbear. I am afraid of applications, which many are too ready to make, and for which I should be sorry to give any just occasion.

I have been explaining to you the nature and expressions of a just regard to our country. Give me leave to exhort you to examine your conduct by what I have been saying. You love your country, and desire its happiness; and, without doubt, you have the greatest reason for loving it. It has been long a very distinguished and favoured country. Often has God appeared for it and delivered it. Let us study to shew ourselves worthy of the favour shewn us.—Do you practise virtue yourselves, and study to promote it in others? Do you obey the laws of your country, and aim at doing your part towards maintaining and perpetuating its privileges? Do you always give your vote on the side of public liberty; and are you ready to pour out your blood in its defence? Do you look up to God for the continuance of his favour to your country, and pray for its prosperity; preserving, at the same time, a strict regard to the rights of other countries, and always considering yourselves more as citizens of the world than as members of any particular community?—If this is your temper and conduct you are blessings to your country, and were all like you, this world would soon be a heaven.

I am addressing myself to Christians. Let me, therefore, mention to you the example of our blessed Saviour. I have observed, at the beginning of this discourse, that he did not inculcate upon his hearers the love of their country, or take any notice of it as a part of our duty. Instead of doing this, I observed that he taught the obligation to love all mankind, and recommended universal benevolence, as (next to the love of God) our first duty; and, I think, I also proved to you, that this, in the circumstances of the world at that time, was an instance of incomparable wisdom and goodness in his instructions. But we must not infer from hence, that he did not include the love of our country in the number of our duties. He has shewn the contrary by his example. It appears that he possessed a particular affection for his country, though a very wicked country. We read in Luke x. 42, that when, upon approaching Jerusalem, in one of his last journies to it, he beheld it, he wept over it, and said; Oh! that thou hadst known (even thou, at least in this thy day) the things that belong to thy peace.— What a tender solicitude about his country does the lamentation over Jerusalem imply, which is recorded in the same gospel, chap. xiii. and 34. Oh! Jerusalem, Jerusalem, thou that killest the prophets, and stonest them who are sent to thee, how often would I have gathered thy children together, as a hen gathereth her brood under her wings, but ye would not.

It may not be improper farther to mention the love St. Paul expressed for his country, when he declared, that, for the sake of his brethren and kinsmen, he could even wish himself accursed from Christ.(Rom. ix. 3.) The original words are an Anathema from Christ; and his meaning is, that he could have been contented to suffer himself the calamities which were coming on the Jewish people, were it possible for him, by such a sacrifice of himself, to save them.

It is too evident that the state of this country is such as renders it an object of concern and anxiety. It wants (I have shewn you) the grand security of public liberty. Increasing luxury has multiplied abuses in it. A monstrous weight of debt is crippling it. Vice and venality are bringing down upon it God's displeasure. That spirit to which it owes its distinctions is declining*; and some late events seem to prove that it is becoming every day more reconcileable to encroachments on the securities of its liberties†.—It wants, therefore, your patriotic services; and, for the sake of the distinctions it has so long enjoyed; for the sake of our brethren and companions, and all that should be dear to a free people, we ought to do our utmost to save it from the dangers that threaten it; remembering, that by acting thus, we shall promote, in the best manner, our own private interest, as well as the interest of our country; for when the community prospers, the individuals that compose it must prosper with it.—But, should that not happen, or should we even suffer in our secular interest by our endeavours to promote the interest of our country, we shall feel a satisfaction in our own breasts which is preferable to all this world can give; and we shall enjoy the transporting hope of soon becoming members of a perfect community in the heavens, and having an entrance ministered to us, abundantly into the everlasting kingdom of our Lord and Saviour Jesus Christ.

You may reasonably expect that I should now close this address to you. But I cannot yet dismiss you. I must not conclude without recalling, particularly, to your recollection, a consideration to which I have more than once alluded, and which, probably, your thoughts have been all along anticipating: A consideration with which my mind is impressed more than I can express. I mean, the consideration of the favourableness of the present times to all exertions in the cause of public liberty.

What an eventful period is this! I am thankful that I have lived to it; and I could almost say, Lord, now lettest thou thy servant depart in peace, for mine eyes have seen thy salvation. I have lived to see a diffusion of knowledge, which has undermined superstition and error—I have lived to see the rights of men better understood than ever; and nations panting for liberty, which seemed to have lost the idea of it.—I have lived to see Thirty Millions of people, indignant and resolute, spurning at slavery, and demanding liberty with an irresistible voice; their king led in triumph, and an arbitrary monarch surrendering himself to his subjects.—After sharing in the benefits of one Revolution, I have been spared to be a witness to two other Revolutions, both glorious.—And now, methinks, I see the ardor for liberty catching and spreading; a general amendment beginning in human affairs; the dominion of kings changed for the dominion of laws, and the dominion of priests giving way to the dominion of reason and conscience.

Be encouraged, all ye friends of freedom, and writers in its defence! The times are auspicious. Your labours have not been in vain. Behold kingdoms, admonished by you, starting from sleep, breaking their fetters, and claiming justice from their oppressors! Behold, the light you have struck out, after setting America free, reflected to France, and there kindled into a blaze that lays despotism in ashes, and warms and illuminates Europe!

Tremble all ye oppressors of the world! Take warning all ye supporters of slavish governments, and slavish hierarchies! Call no more (absurdly and wickedly) Reformation, innovation. You cannot now hold the world in darkness. Struggle no longer against increasing light and liberality. Restore to mankind their rights; and consent to the correction of abuses, before they and you are destroyed together.

FINIS.

Reflections on the Revolution in France (1790)

Edmund Burke (1729-1797)

IT MAY NOT BE UNNECESSARY to inform the reader that the following Reflections had their origin in a correspondence between the Author and a very young gentleman at Paris, who did him the honor of desiring his opinion upon the important transactions which then, and ever since, have so much occupied the attention of all men. An answer was written sometime in the month of October 1789, but it was kept back upon prudential considerations. That letter is alluded to in the beginning of the following sheets. It has been since forwarded to the person to whom it was addressed. The reasons for the delay in sending it were assigned in a short letter to the same gentleman. This produced on his part a new and pressing application for the Author's sentiments.

The Author began a second and more full discussion on the subject. This he had some thoughts of publishing early in the last spring; but, the matter gaining upon him, he found that what he had undertaken not only far exceeded the measure of a letter, but that its importance required rather a more detailed consideration than at that time he had any leisure to bestow upon it. However, having thrown down his first thoughts in the form of a letter, and, indeed, when he sat down to write, having intended it for a private letter, he found it difficult to change the form of address when his sentiments had grown into a greater extent and had received another direction. A different plan, he is sensible, might be more favorable to a commodious division and distribution of his matter.

Dear Sir,

You are pleased to call again, and with some earnestness, for my thoughts on the late proceedings in France. I will not give you reason to imagine that I think my sentiments of such value as to wish myself to be solicited about them. They are of too little consequence to be very anxiously either communicated or withheld. It was from attention to you, and to you only, that I hesitated at the time when you first desired to receive them. In the first letter I had the honor to write to you, and which at length I send, I wrote neither for, nor from, any description of men, nor shall I in this.

My errors, if any, are my own. My reputation alone is to answer for them.

You see, Sir, by the long letter I have transmitted to you, that though I do most heartily wish that France may be animated by a spirit of rational liberty, and that I think you bound, in all honest policy, to provide a permanent body in which that spirit may reside, and an effectual organ by which it may act, it is my misfortune to entertain great doubts concerning several material points in your late transactions.

YOU IMAGINED, WHEN YOU WROTE LAST, that I might possibly be reckoned among the approvers of certain proceedings in France, from the solemn public seal of sanction they have received from two clubs of gentlemen in London, called the Constitutional Society and the Revolution Society.

I certainly have the honor to belong to more clubs than one, in which the constitution of this kingdom and the principles of the glorious Revolution are held in high reverence, and I reckon myself among the most forward in my zeal for maintaining that constitution and those principles in their utmost purity and vigor. It is because I do so, that I think it necessary for me that there should be no mistake. Those who cultivate the memory of our Revolution and those who are attached to the constitution of this kingdom will take good care how they are involved with persons who, under the pretext of zeal toward the Revolution and constitution, too frequently wander from their true principles and are ready on every occasion to depart from the firm but cautious and deliberate spirit which produced the one, and which presides in the other. Before I proceed to answer the more material particulars in your letter, I shall beg leave to give you such information as I have been able to obtain of the two clubs which have thought proper, as bodies, to interfere in the concerns of France, first assuring you that I am not, and that I have never been, a member of either of those societies.

The first, calling itself the Constitutional Society, or Society for Constitutional Information, or by some such title, is, I believe, of seven or eight years standing. The institution of this society appears to be of a charitable and so far of a laudable nature; it was intended for the circulation, at the expense of the members, of many books which few others would be at the expense of buying, and which might lie on the hands of the booksellers, to the great loss of an useful body of men. Whether the books, so charitably circulated, were ever as charitably read is more than I know. Possibly several of them have been exported to France and, like goods not in request here, may with you have found a market. I have heard much talk of the lights to be drawn from books that are sent from hence. What improvements they have had in their passage (as it is said some liquors are meliorated by crossing the sea) I cannot tell; but I never heard a man of common judgment or the least degree of information speak a word in praise of the greater part of the publications circulated by that society, nor have their proceedings been accounted, except by some of themselves, as of any serious consequence.

Your National Assembly seems to entertain much the same opinion that I do of this poor charitable club. As a nation, you reserved the whole stock of your eloquent acknowledgments for the Revolution Society, when their fellows in the Constitutional were, in equity, entitled to some share. Since you have selected the Revolution Society as the great object of your national thanks and praises, you will think me excusable in making its late conduct the subject of my observations. The National Assembly of France has given importance to these gentlemen by adopting them; and they return the favor by acting as a committee in England for extending the principles of the National Assembly. Henceforward we must consider them as a kind of privileged persons, as no inconsiderable members in the diplomatic body. This is one among the revolutions which have given splendor to obscurity, and distinction to undiscerned merit. Until very lately I do not recollect to have heard of this club. I am quite sure that it never occupied a moment of my thoughts, nor, I believe, those of any person out of their own set. I find, upon inquiry, that on the anniversary of the Revolution in 1688, a club of dissenters, but of what denomination I know not, have long had the custom of hearing a sermon in one of their churches; and that afterwards they spent the day cheerfully, as other clubs do, at the tavern. But I never heard that any public measure or political system, much less that the merits of the constitution of any foreign nation, had been the subject of a formal proceeding at their festivals, until, to my inexpressible surprise, I found them in a sort of public capacity, by a congratulatory address, giving an authoritative sanction to the proceedings of the National Assembly in France.

In the ancient principles and conduct of the club, so far at least as they were declared, I see nothing to which I could take exception. I think it very probable that for some purpose new members may have entered among them, and that some truly Christian politicians, who love to dispense benefits but are careful to conceal the hand which distributes the dole, may have made them the instruments of their pious designs. Whatever I may have reason to suspect concerning private management, I shall speak of nothing as of a certainty but what is public.

For one, I should be sorry to be thought, directly or indirectly, concerned in their proceedings. I certainly take my full share, along with the rest of the world, in my individual and private capacity, in speculating on what has been done or is doing on the public stage in any place ancient or modern; in the republic of Rome or the republic of Paris; but having no general apostolical mission, being a citizen of a particular state and being bound up, in a considerable degree, by its public will, I should think it at least improper and irregular for me to open a formal public correspondence with the actual government of a foreign nation, without the express authority of the government under which I live.

I should be still more unwilling to enter into that correspondence under anything like an equivocal description, which to many, unacquainted with our usages, might make the address, in which I joined, appear as the act of persons in some sort of corporate capacity acknowledged by the laws of this kingdom and authorized to speak the sense of some part of it. On account of the ambiguity and uncertainty of unauthorized general descriptions, and of the deceit which may be practiced under them, and not from mere formality, the House of Commons would reject the most sneaking petition for the most trifling object, under that mode of signature to which you have thrown open the folding doors of your presence chamber, and have ushered into your National Assembly with as much ceremony and parade, and with as great a bustle of applause, as if you have been visited by the whole representative majesty of the whole English nation. If what this society has thought proper to send forth had been a piece of argument, it would have signified little whose argument it was. It would be neither the more nor the less convincing on account of the party it came from. But this is only a vote and resolution. It stands solely on authority; and in this case it is the mere authority of individuals, few of whom appear. Their signatures ought, in my opinion, to have been annexed to their instrument. The world would then have the means of knowing how many they are; who they are; and of what value their opinions may be, from their personal abilities, from their knowledge, their experience, or their lead and authority in this state. To me, who am but a plain man, the proceeding looks a little too refined and too ingenious; it has too much the air of a political strategem adopted for the sake of giving, under a high-sounding name, an importance to the public declarations of this club which, when the matter came to be closely inspected, they did not altogether so well deserve. It is a policy that has very much the complexion of a fraud.

I flatter myself that I love a manly, moral, regulated liberty as well as any gentleman of that society, be he who he will; and perhaps I have given as good proofs of my attachment to that cause in the whole course of my public conduct. I think I envy liberty as little as they do to any other nation. But I cannot stand forward and give praise or blame to anything which relates to human actions, and human concerns, on a simple view of the object, as it stands stripped of every relation, in all the nakedness and solitude of metaphysical abstraction. Circumstances (which with some gentlemen pass for nothing) give in reality to every political principle its distinguishing color and discriminating effect. The circumstances are what render every civil and political scheme beneficial or noxious to mankind. Abstractedly speaking, government, as well as liberty, is good; yet could I, in common sense, ten years ago, have felicitated France on her enjoyment of a government (for she then had a government) without inquiry what the nature of that government was, or how it was administered? Can I now congratulate the same nation upon its freedom? Is it because liberty in the abstract may be classed amongst the blessings of mankind, that I am seriously to felicitate a madman, who has escaped from the protecting restraint and wholesome darkness of his cell, on his restoration to the enjoyment of light and liberty? Am I to congratulate a highwayman and murderer who has broke prison upon the recovery of his natural rights? This would be to act over again the scene of the criminals condemned to the galleys, and their heroic deliverer, the metaphysic Knight of the Sorrowful Countenance.

When I see the spirit of liberty in action, I see a strong principle at work; and this, for a while, is all I can possibly know of it. The wild gas, the fixed air, is plainly broke loose; but we ought to suspend our judgment until the first effervescence is a little subsided, till the liquor is cleared, and until we see something deeper than the agitation of a troubled and frothy surface. I must be tolerably sure, before I venture publicly to congratulate men upon a blessing, that they have really received one. Flattery corrupts both the receiver and the giver, and adulation is not of more service to the people than to kings. I should, therefore, suspend my congratulations on the new liberty of France until I was informed how it had been combined with government, with public force, with the discipline and obedience of armies, with the collection of an effective and well-distributed revenue, with morality and religion, with the solidity of property, with peace and order, with civil and social manners. All these (in their way) are good things, too, and without them liberty is not a benefit whilst it lasts, and is not likely to continue long. The effect of liberty to individuals is that they may do what they please; we ought to see what it will please them to do, before we risk congratulations which may be soon turned into complaints. Prudence would dictate this in the case of separate, insulated, private men, but liberty, when men act in bodies, is power. Considerate people, before they declare themselves, will observe the use which is made of power and particularly of so trying a thing as new power in new persons of whose principles, tempers, and dispositions they have little or no experience, and in situations where those who appear the most stirring in the scene may possibly not be the real movers.

ALL these considerations, however, were below the transcendental dignity of the Revolution Society. Whilst I continued in the country, from whence I had the honor of writing to you, I had but an imperfect idea of their transactions. On my coming to town, I sent for an account of their proceedings, which had been published by their authority, containing a sermon of Dr. Price, with the Duke de Rochefoucault's and the Archbishop of Aix's letter, and several other documents annexed. The whole of that publication, with the manifest design of connecting the affairs of France with those of England by drawing us into an imitation of the conduct of the National Assembly, gave me a considerable degree of uneasiness. The effect of that conduct upon the power, credit, prosperity, and tranquility of France became every day more evident. The form of constitution to be settled for its future polity became more clear. We are now in a condition to discern, with tolerable exactness, the true nature of the object held up to our imitation. If the prudence of reserve and decorum dictates silence in some circumstances, in others prudence of a higher order may justify us in speaking our thoughts. The beginnings of confusion with us in England are at present feeble enough, but, with you, we have seen an infancy still more feeble growing by moments into a strength to heap mountains upon mountains and to wage war with heaven itself. Whenever our neighbor's house is on fire, it cannot be amiss for the engines to play a little on our own. Better to be despised for too anxious apprehensions than ruined by too confident a security.

Solicitous chiefly for the peace of my own country, but by no means unconcerned for yours, I wish to communicate more largely what was at first intended only for your private satisfaction. I shall still keep your affairs in my eye and continue to address myself to you. Indulging myself in the freedom of epistolary intercourse, I beg leave to throw out my thoughts and express my feelings just as they arise in my mind, with very little attention to formal method. I set out with the proceedings of the Revolution Society, but I shall not confine myself to them. Is it possible I should? It appears to me as if I were in a great crisis, not of the affairs of France alone, but of all Europe, perhaps of more than Europe. All circumstances taken together, the French revolution is the most astonishing that has hitherto happened in the world. The most wonderful things are brought about, in many instances by means the most absurd and ridiculous, in the most ridiculous modes, and apparently by the most contemptible instruments. Everything seems out of nature in this strange chaos of levity and ferocity, and of all sorts of crimes jumbled together with all sorts of follies. In viewing this monstrous tragicomic scene, the most opposite passions necessarily succeed and sometimes mix with each other in the mind: alternate contempt and indignation, alternate laughter and tears, alternate scorn and horror.

It cannot, however, be denied that to some this strange scene appeared in quite another point of view. Into them it inspired no other sentiments than those of exultation and rapture. They saw nothing in what has been done in France but a firm and temperate exertion of freedom, so consistent, on the whole, with morals and with piety as to make it deserving not only of the secular applause of dashing Machiavellian politicians, but to render it a fit theme for all the devout effusions of sacred eloquence.

On the forenoon of the fourth of November last, Doctor Richard Price, a non-conforming minister of eminence, preached, at the dissenting meeting house of the Old Jewry, to his club or society, a very extraordinary miscellaneous sermon, in which there are some good moral and religious sentiments, and not ill expressed, mixed up in a sort of porridge of various political opinions and reflections; but the Revolution in France is the grand ingredient in the cauldron. I consider the address transmitted by the Revolution Society to the National Assembly, through Earl Stanhope, as originating in the principles of the sermon and as a corollary from them. It was moved by the preacher of that discourse. It was passed by those who came reeking from the effect of the sermon without any censure or qualification, expressed or implied. If, however, any of the gentlemen concerned shall wish to separate the sermon from the resolution, they know how to acknowledge the one and to disavow the other. They may do it: I cannot.

For my part, I looked on that sermon as the public declaration of a man much connected with literary caballers and intriguing philosophers, with political theologians and theological politicians both at home and abroad. I know they set him up as a sort of oracle, because, with the best intentions in the world, he naturally philippizes and chants his prophetic song in exact unison with their designs.

That sermon is in a strain which I believe has not been heard in this kingdom, in any of the pulpits which are tolerated or encouraged in it, since the year 1648, when a predecessor of Dr. Price, the Rev. Hugh Peters, made the vault of the king's own chapel at St. James's ring with the honor and privilege of the saints, who, with the "high praises of God in their mouths, and a two-edged sword in their hands, were to execute judgment on the heathen, and punishments upon the people; to bind their kings with chains, and their nobles with fetters of iron".[1] Few harangues from the pulpit, except in the days of your league in France or in the days of our Solemn League and Covenant in England, have ever breathed less of the spirit of moderation than this lecture in the Old Jewry. Supposing, however, that something like moderation were visible in this political sermon, yet politics and the pulpit are terms that have little agreement. No sound ought to be heard in the church but the healing voice of Christian charity. The cause of civil liberty and civil government gains as little as that of religion by this confusion of duties. Those who quit their proper character to assume what does not belong to them are, for the greater part, ignorant both of the character they leave and of the character they assume. Wholly unacquainted with the world in which they are so fond of meddling, and inexperienced in all its affairs on which they pronounce with so much confidence, they have nothing of politics but the passions they excite. Surely the church is a place where one day's truce ought to be allowed to the dissensions and animosities of mankind.

This pulpit style, revived after so long a discontinuance, had to me the air of novelty, and of a novelty not wholly without danger. I do not charge this danger equally to every part of the discourse. The hint given to a noble and reverend lay divine, who is supposed high in office in one of our universities, ⌐ and other lay divines "of rank and literature" may be proper and seasonable, though somewhat new. If the noble Seekers should find nothing to satisfy their pious fancies in the old staple of the national church, or in all the rich variety to be found in the well-assorted warehouses of the dissenting congregations, Dr. Price advises them to improve upon non-conformity and to set up, each of them, a separate meeting house upon his own particular principles.⌐ It is somewhat remarkable that this reverend divine should be so earnest for setting up new churches and so perfectly indifferent concerning the doctrine which may be taught in them. His zeal is of a curious character. It is not for the propagation of his own opinions, but of any opinions. It is not for the diffusion of truth, but for the spreading of contradiction. Let the noble teachers but dissent, it is no matter from whom or from what. This great point once secured, it is taken for granted their religion will be rational and manly. I doubt whether religion would reap all the benefits which the calculating divine computes from this "great company of great preachers". It would certainly be a valuable addition of nondescripts to the ample collection of known classes, genera and species, which at present beautify the hortus siccus of dissent. A sermon from a noble duke, or a noble marquis, or a noble earl, or baron bold would certainly increase and diversify the amusements of this town, which begins to grow satiated with the uniform round of its vapid dissipations. I should only stipulate that these new Mess-Johns in robes and coronets should keep some sort of bounds in the democratic and leveling principles which are expected from their titled pulpits. The new evangelists will, I dare say, disappoint the hopes that are conceived of them. They will not become, literally as well as figuratively, polemic divines, nor be disposed so to drill their congregations that they may, as in former blessed times, preach their doctrines to regiments of dragoons and corps of infantry and artillery. Such arrangements, however favorable to the cause of compulsory freedom, civil and religious, may not be equally conducive to the national tranquility. These few restrictions I hope are no great stretches of intolerance, no very violent exertions of despotism.

BUT I may say of our preacher "utinam nugis tota illa dedisset tempora saevitiae". — All things in this his fulminating bull are not of so innoxious a tendency. His doctrines affect our constitution in its vital parts. He tells the Revolution Society in this political sermon that his Majesty "is almost the only lawful king in the world because the only one who owes his crown to the choice of his people." As to the kings of the world, all of whom (except one) this archpontiff of the rights of men, with all the plenitude and with more than the boldness of the papal deposing power in its meridian fervor of the twelfth century, puts into one sweeping clause of ban and anathema and proclaims usurpers by circles of longitude and latitude, over the whole globe, it behooves them to consider how they admit into their territories these apostolic missionaries who are to tell their subjects they are not lawful kings. That is their concern. It is ours, as a domestic interest of some moment, seriously to consider the solidity of the only principle upon which these gentlemen acknowledge a king of Great Britain to be entitled to their allegiance.

This doctrine, as applied to the prince now on the British throne, either is nonsense and therefore neither true nor false, or it affirms a most unfounded, dangerous, illegal, and unconstitutional position. According to this spiritual doctor of politics, if his Majesty does not owe his crown to the choice of his people, he is no lawful king. Now nothing can be more untrue than that the crown of this kingdom is so held by his Majesty. Therefore, if you follow their rule, the king of Great Britain, who most certainly does not owe his high office to any form of popular election, is in no respect better than the rest of the gang of usurpers who reign, or rather rob, all over the face of this our miserable world without any sort of right or title to the allegiance of their people. The policy of this general doctrine, so qualified, is evident enough. The propagators of this political gospel are in hopes that their abstract principle (their principle that a popular choice is necessary to the legal existence of the sovereign magistracy) would be overlooked, whilst the king of Great Britain was not affected by it. In the meantime the ears of their congregations would be gradually habituated to it, as if it were a first principle admitted without dispute. For the present it would only operate as a theory, pickled in the preserving juices of pulpit eloquence, and laid by for future use. Condo et compono quae mox depromere possim. By this policy, whilst our government is soothed with a reservation in its favor, to which it has no claim, the security which it has in common with all governments, so far as opinion is security, is taken away.

Thus these politicians proceed whilst little notice is taken of their doctrines; but when they come to be examined upon the plain meaning of their words and the direct tendency of their doctrines, then equivocations and slippery constructions come into play. When they say the king owes his crown to the choice of his people and is therefore the only lawful sovereign in the world, they will perhaps tell us they mean to say no more than that some of the king's predecessors have been called to the throne by some sort of choice, and therefore he owes his crown to the choice of his people. Thus, by a miserable subterfuge, they hope to render their proposition safe by rendering it nugatory. They are welcome to the asylum they seek for their offense, since they take refuge in their folly. For if you admit this interpretation, how does their idea of election differ from our idea of inheritance?

And how does the settlement of the crown in the Brunswick line derived from James the First come to legalize our monarchy rather than that of any of the neighboring countries? At some time or other, to be sure, all the beginners of dynasties were chosen by those who called them to govern. There is ground enough for the opinion that all the kingdoms of Europe were, at a remote period, elective, with more or fewer limitations in the objects of choice. But whatever kings might have been here or elsewhere a thousand years ago, or in whatever manner the ruling dynasties of England or France may have begun, the king of Great Britain is, at this day, king by a fixed rule of succession according to the laws of his country; and whilst the legal conditions of the compact of sovereignty are performed by him (as they are performed), he holds his crown in contempt of the choice of the Revolution Society, who have not a single vote for a king amongst them, either individually or collectively, though I make no doubt they would soon erect themselves into an electoral college if things were ripe to give effect to their claim. His Majesty's heirs and successors, each in his time and order, will come to the crown with the same contempt of their choice with which his Majesty has succeeded to that he wears.

Whatever may be the success of evasion in explaining away the gross error of fact, which supposes that his Majesty (though he holds it in concurrence with the wishes) owes his crown to the choice of his people, yet nothing can evade their full explicit declaration concerning the principle of a right in the people to choose; which right is directly maintained and tenaciously adhered to. All the oblique insinuations concerning election bottom in this proposition and are referable to it. Lest the foundation of the king's exclusive legal title should pass for a mere rant of adulatory freedom, the political divine proceeds dogmatically to assert that, by the principles of the Revolution, the people of England have acquired three fundamental rights, all which, with him, compose one system and lie together in one short sentence, namely, that we have acquired a right:

(1) to choose our own governors.

(2) to cashier them for misconduct.

(3) to frame a government for ourselves.

This new and hitherto unheard-of bill of rights, though made in the name of the whole people, belongs to those gentlemen and their faction only. The body of the people of England have no share in it. They utterly disclaim it. They will resist the practical assertion of it with their lives and fortunes. They are bound to do so by the laws of their country made at the time of that very Revolution which is appealed to in favor of the fictitious rights claimed by the Society which abuses its name.

THESE GENTLEMEN OF THE OLD JEWRY, in all their reasonings on the Revolution of 1688, have a revolution which happened in England about forty years before and the late French revolution, so much before their eyes and in their hearts that they are constantly confounding all the three together. It is necessary that we should separate what they confound. We must recall their erring fancies to the acts of the Revolution which we revere, for the discovery of its true principles. If the principles of the Revolution of 1688 are anywhere to be found, it is in the statute called the Declaration of Right. In that most wise, sober, and considerate declaration, drawn up by great lawyers and great statesmen, and not by warm and inexperienced enthusiasts, not one word is said, nor one suggestion made, of a general right "to choose our own governors, to cashier them for misconduct, and to form a government for ourselves".

This Declaration of Right (the act of the 1st of William and Mary, sess. 2, ch. 2) is the cornerstone of our constitution as reinforced, explained, improved, and in its fundamental principles for ever settled. It is called, "An Act for declaring the rights and liberties of the subject, and for settling the succession of the crown". You will observe that these rights and this succession are declared in one body and bound indissolubly together.

A few years after this period, a second opportunity offered for asserting a right of election to the crown. On the prospect of a total failure of issue from King William, and from the Princess, afterwards Queen Anne, the consideration of the settlement of the crown and of a further security for the liberties of the people again came before the legislature. Did they this second time make any provision for legalizing the crown on the spurious revolution principles of the Old Jewry? No. They followed the principles which prevailed in the Declaration of Right, indicating with more precision the persons who were to inherit in the Protestant line. This act also incorporated, by the same policy, our liberties and an hereditary succession in the same act. Instead of a right to choose our own governors, they declared that the succession in that line (the Protestant line drawn from James the First), was absolutely necessary "for the peace, quiet, and security of the realm", and that it was equally urgent on them "to maintain a certainty in the succession thereof, to which the subjects may safely have recourse for their protection". Both these acts, in which are heard the unerring, unambiguous oracles of revolution policy, instead of countenancing the delusive, gipsy predictions of a "right to choose our governors", prove to a demonstration how totally adverse the wisdom of the nation was from turning a case of necessity into a rule of law.

Unquestionably, there was at the Revolution, in the person of King William, a small and a temporary deviation from the strict order of a regular hereditary succession; but it is against all genuine principles of jurisprudence to draw a principle from a law made in a special case and regarding an individual person. Privilegium non transit in exemplum. If ever there was a time favorable for establishing the principle that a king of popular choice was the only legal king, without all doubt it was at the Revolution. It's not being done at that time is a proof that the nation was of opinion it ought not to be done at any time. There is no person so completely ignorant of our history as not to know that the majority in parliament of both parties were so little disposed to anything resembling that principle that at first they were determined to place the vacant crown, not on the head of the Prince of Orange, but on that of his wife Mary, daughter of King James, the eldest born of the issue of that king, which they acknowledged as undoubtedly his. It would be to repeat a very trite story, to recall to your

Eighteenth Century Blogosphere

memory all those circumstances which demonstrated that their accepting King William was not properly a choice; but to all those who did not wish, in effect, to recall King James or to deluge their country in blood and again to bring their religion, laws, and liberties into the peril they had just escaped, it was an act of necessity, in the strictest moral sense in which necessity can be taken.

In the very act in which for a time, and in a single case, parliament departed from the strict order of inheritance in favor of a prince who, though not next, was, however, very near in the line of succession, it is curious to observe how Lord Somers, who drew the bill called the Declaration of Right, has comported himself on that delicate occasion. It is curious to observe with what address this temporary solution of continuity is kept from the eye, whilst all that could be found in this act of necessity to countenance the idea of an hereditary succession is brought forward, and fostered, and made the most of, by this great man and by the legislature who followed him. Quitting the dry, imperative style of an act of parliament, he makes the Lords and Commons fall to a pious, legislative ejaculation and declare that they consider it "as a marvellous providence and merciful goodness of God to this nation to preserve their said Majesties' royal persons most happily to reign over us on the throne of their ancestors, for which, from the bottom of their hearts, they return their humblest thanks and praises". — The legislature plainly had in view the act of recognition of the first of Queen Elizabeth, chap. 3rd, and of that of James the First, chap. 1st, both acts strongly declaratory of the inheritable nature of the crown; and in many parts they follow, with a nearly literal precision, the words and even the form of thanksgiving which is found in these old declaratory statutes.

The two Houses, in the act of King William, did not thank God that they had found a fair opportunity to assert a right to choose their own governors, much less to make an election the only lawful title to the crown. Their having been in a condition to avoid the very appearance of it, as much as possible, was by them considered as a providential escape. They threw a politic, well-wrought veil over every circumstance tending to weaken the rights which in the meliorated order of succession they meant to perpetuate, or which might furnish a precedent for any future departure from what they had then settled forever. Accordingly, that they might not relax the nerves of their monarchy, and that they might preserve a close conformity to the practice of their ancestors, as it appeared in the declaratory statutes of Queen Mary and Queen Elizabeth, in the next clause they vest, by recognition, in their Majesties all the legal prerogatives of the crown, declaring "that in them they are most fully, rightfully, and entirely invested, incorporated, united, and annexed". In the clause which follows, for preventing questions by reason of any pretended titles to the crown, they declare (observing also in this the traditionary language, along with the traditionary policy of the nation, and repeating as from a rubric the language of the preceding acts of Elizabeth and James,) that on the preserving "a certainty in the SUCCESSION thereof, the unity, peace, and tranquillity of this nation doth, under God, wholly depend".

They knew that a doubtful title of succession would but too much resemble an election, and that an election would be utterly destructive of the "unity, peace, and tranquillity of this nation", which they thought to be considerations of some moment. To provide for these objects and, therefore, to exclude forever the Old Jewry doctrine of "a right to choose our own governors", they follow with a clause containing a most solemn pledge, taken from the preceding act of Queen Elizabeth, as solemn a pledge as ever was or can be given in favor of an hereditary succession, and as solemn a renunciation as could be made of the principles by this Society imputed to them: The Lords spiritual and temporal, and Commons, do, in the name of all the people aforesaid, most humbly and faithfully submit themselves, their heirs and posterities for ever; and do faithfully promise that they will stand to maintain, and defend their said Majesties, and also the limitation of the crown, herein specified and contained, to the utmost of their powers, etc. etc.

So far is it from being true that we acquired a right by the Revolution to elect our kings that, if we had possessed it before, the English nation did at that time most solemnly renounce and abdicate it, for themselves and for all their posterity forever.

These gentlemen may value themselves as much as they please on their whig principles, but I never desire to be thought a better whig than Lord Somers, or to understand the principles of the Revolution better than those, by whom it was brought about, or to read in the Declaration of Right any mysteries unknown to those whose penetrating style has engraved in our ordinances, and in our hearts, the words and spirit of that immortal law.

It is true that, aided with the powers derived from force and opportunity, the nation was at that time, in some sense, free to take what course it pleased for filling the throne, but only free to do so upon the same grounds on which they might have wholly abolished their monarchy and every other part of their constitution. However, they did not think such bold changes within their commission. It is indeed difficult, perhaps impossible, to give limits to the mere abstract competence of the supreme power, such as was exercised by parliament at that time, but the limits of a moral competence subjecting, even in powers more indisputably sovereign, occasional will to permanent reason and to the steady maxims of faith, justice, and fixed fundamental policy, are perfectly intelligible and perfectly binding upon those who exercise any authority, under any name or under any title, in the state. The House of Lords, for instance, is not morally competent to dissolve the House of Commons, no, nor even to dissolve itself, nor to abdicate, if it would, its portion in the legislature of the kingdom. Though a king may abdicate for his own person, he cannot abdicate for the monarchy. By as strong, or by a stronger reason, the House of Commons cannot renounce its share of authority. The engagement and pact of society, which generally goes by the name of the constitution, forbids such invasion and such surrender. The constituent parts of a state are obliged to hold their public faith with each other and with all those who derive any serious interest under their engagements, as much as the whole state is bound to keep its faith with separate communities. Otherwise competence and power would soon be confounded and no law be left but the will of a prevailing force. On this principle the succession of the crown has always been what it now is, an hereditary succession by law; in the old line it was a succession by the common law; in the new, by the statute law operating on the principles of the common law, not changing the substance, but regulating the mode and describing the persons. Both these descriptions of law are of the same force and are derived from an equal authority emanating from the common agreement and original compact of the state, communi sponsione reipublicae, and as such are equally binding on king and people, too, as long as the terms are observed and they continue the same body politic.

It is far from impossible to reconcile, if we do not suffer ourselves to be entangled in the mazes of metaphysic sophistry, the use both of a fixed rule and an occasional deviation: the sacredness of an hereditary principle of succession in our government with a power of change in its application in cases of extreme emergency. Even in that extremity (if we take the measure of our rights by our exercise of them at the Revolution), the change is to be confined to the peccant part only, to the part which produced the necessary deviation; and even then it is to be effected without a decomposition of the whole civil and political mass for the purpose of originating a new civil order out of the first elements of society.

A state without the means of some change is without the means of its conservation. Without such means it might even risk the loss of that part of the constitution which it wished the most religiously to preserve. The two principles of conservation and correction operated strongly at the two critical periods of the Restoration and Revolution, when England found itself without a king. At both those periods the nation had lost the bond of union in their ancient edifice; they did not, however, dissolve the whole fabric. On the contrary, in both cases they regenerated the deficient part of the old constitution through the parts which were not impaired. They kept these old parts exactly as they were, that the part recovered might be suited to them. They acted by the ancient organized states in the shape of their old organization, and not by the organic moleculae of a disbanded people. At no time, perhaps, did the sovereign legislature manifest a more tender regard to that fundamental principle of British constitutional policy than at the time of the Revolution, when it deviated from the direct line of hereditary succession. The crown was carried somewhat out of the line in which it had before moved, but the new line was derived from the same stock. It was still a line of hereditary descent, still an hereditary descent in the same blood, though an hereditary descent qualified with Protestantism. When the legislature altered the direction, but kept the principle, they showed that they held it inviolable.

On this principle, the law of inheritance had admitted some amendment in the old time, and long before the era of the Revolution. Sometime after the Conquest, great questions arose upon the legal principles of hereditary descent. It became a matter of doubt whether the heir per capita or the heir per stirpes was to succeed; but whether the heir per capita gave way when the heirdom per stirpes took place, or the Catholic heir when the Protestant was preferred, the inheritable principle survived with a sort of immortality through all transmigrations — multosque per annos stat fortuna domus, et avi numerantur avorum. This is the spirit of our constitution, not only in its settled course, but in all its revolutions. Whoever came in, or however he came in, whether he obtained the crown by law or by force, the hereditary succession was either continued or adopted.

The gentlemen of the Society for Revolution see nothing in that of 1688 but the deviation from the constitution; and they take the deviation from the principle for the principle. They have little regard to the obvious consequences of their doctrine, though they must see that it leaves positive authority in very few of the positive institutions of this country. When such an unwarrantable maxim is once established, that no throne is lawful but the elective, no one act of the princes who preceded this era of fictitious election can be valid. Do these theorists mean to imitate some of their predecessors who dragged the bodies of our ancient sovereigns out of the quiet of their tombs? Do they mean to attaint and disable backward all the kings that have reigned before the Revolution, and consequently to stain the throne of England with the blot of a continual usurpation? Do they mean to invalidate, annul, or to call into question, together with the titles of the whole line of our kings, that great body of our statute law which passed under those whom they treat as usurpers, to annul laws of inestimable value to our liberties ? of as great value at least as any which have passed at or since the period of the Revolution? If kings who did not owe their crown to the choice of their people had no title to make laws, what will become of the statute de tallagio non concedendo? — of the petition of right? — of the act of habeas corpus? Do these new doctors of the rights of men presume to assert that King James the Second, who came to the crown as next of blood, according to the rules of a then unqualified succession, was not to all intents and purposes a lawful king of England before he had done any of those acts which were justly construed into an abdication of his crown? If he was not, much trouble in parliament might have been saved at the period these gentlemen commemorate. But King James was a bad king with a good title, and not an usurper. The princes who succeeded, according to the act of parliament which settled the crown on the Electress Sophia and on her descendants, being Protestants, came in as much by a title of inheritance as King James did. He came in according to the law as it stood at his accession to the crown; and the princes of the House of Brunswick came to the inheritance of the crown, not by election, but by the law as it stood at their several accessions of Protestant descent and inheritance, as I hope I have shown sufficiently.

The law by which this royal family is specifically destined to the succession is the act of the 12th and 13th of King William. The terms of this act bind "us and our heirs, and our posterity, to them, their heirs, and their posterity", being Protestants, to the end of time, in the same words as the Declaration of Right had bound us to the heirs of King William and Queen Mary. It therefore secures both an hereditary crown and an hereditary allegiance. On what ground, except the constitutional policy of forming an establishment to secure that kind of succession which is to preclude a choice of the people forever, could the legislature have fastidiously rejected the fair and abundant choice which our country presented to them and searched in strange lands for a foreign princess from whose womb the line of our future rulers were to derive their title to govern millions of men through a series of ages?

The Princess Sophia was named in the act of settlement of the 12th and 13th of King William for a stock and root of inheritance to our kings, and not for her merits as a temporary administratrix of a power which she might not, and in fact did not, herself ever exercise. She was adopted for one reason, and for one only, because, says the act, "the most excellent Princess Sophia, Electress and Duchess Dowager of Hanover, is daughter of the most excellent Princess Elizabeth, late Queen of Bohemia, daughter of our late sovereign lord King James the First, of happy memory, and is hereby declared to be the next in succession in the Protestant line etc., etc., and the crown shall continue to the heirs of her body, being Protestants." This limitation was made by parliament, that through the Princess Sophia an inheritable line not only was to be continued in future, but (what they thought very material) that through her it was to be connected with the old stock of inheritance in King James the First, in order that the monarchy might preserve an unbroken unity through all ages and might be preserved (with safety to our religion) in the old approved mode by descent, in which, if our liberties had been once endangered, they had often, through all storms and struggles of prerogative and privilege, been preserved. They did well. No experience has taught us that in any other course or method than that of an hereditary crown our liberties can be regularly perpetuated and preserved sacred as our hereditary right.

An irregular, convulsive movement may be necessary to throw off an irregular, convulsive disease. But the course of succession is the healthy habit of the British constitution. Was it that the legislature wanted, at the act for the limitation of the crown in the Hanoverian line, drawn through the female descendants of James the First, a due sense of the inconveniences of having two or three, or possibly more, foreigners in succession to the British throne? No! — they had a due sense of the evils which might happen from such foreign rule, and more than a due sense of them. But a more decisive proof cannot be given of the full conviction of the British nation that the principles of the Revolution did not authorize them to elect kings at their pleasure, and without any attention to the ancient fundamental principles of our government, than their continuing to adopt a plan of hereditary Protestant succession in the old line, with all the dangers and all the inconveniences of its being a foreign line full before their eyes and operating with the utmost force upon their minds.

A few years ago I should be ashamed to overload a matter so capable of supporting itself by the then unnecessary support of any argument; but this seditious, unconstitutional doctrine is now publicly taught, avowed, and printed. The dislike I feel to revolutions, the signals for which have so often been given from pulpits; the spirit of change that is gone abroad; the total contempt which prevails with you, and may come to prevail with us, of all ancient institutions when set in opposition to a present sense of convenience or to the bent of a present inclination: all these considerations make it not unadvisable, in my opinion, to call back our attention to the true principles of our own domestic laws; that you, my French friend, should begin to know, and that we should continue to cherish them. We ought not, on either side of the water, to suffer ourselves to be imposed upon by the counterfeit wares which some persons, by a double fraud, export to you in illicit bottoms as raw commodities of British growth, though wholly alien to our soil, in order afterwards to smuggle them back again into this country, manufactured after the newest Paris fashion of an improved liberty.

The people of England will not ape the fashions they have never tried, nor go back to those which they have found mischievous on trial. They look upon the legal hereditary succession of their crown as among their rights, not as among their wrongs; as a benefit, not as a grievance; as a security for their liberty, not as a badge of servitude. They look on the frame of their commonwealth, such as it stands, to be of inestimable value, and they conceive the undisturbed succession of the crown to be a pledge of the stability and perpetuity of all the other members of our constitution.

I shall beg leave, before I go any further, to take notice of some paltry artifices which the abettors of election, as the only lawful title to the crown, are ready to employ in order to render the support of the just principles of our constitution a task somewhat invidious. These sophisters substitute a fictitious cause and feigned personages, in whose favor they suppose you engaged whenever you defend the inheritable nature of the crown. It is common with them to dispute as if they were in a conflict with some of those exploded fanatics of slavery, who formerly maintained what I believe no creature now maintains, "that the crown is held by divine hereditary and indefeasible right". — These old fanatics of single arbitrary power dogmatized as if hereditary royalty was the only lawful government in the world, just as our new fanatics of popular arbitrary power maintain that a popular election is the sole lawful source of authority. The old prerogative enthusiasts, it is true, did speculate foolishly, and perhaps impiously too, as if monarchy had more of a divine sanction than any other mode of government; and as if a right to govern by inheritance were in strictness indefeasible in every person who should be found in the succession to a throne, and under every circumstance, which no civil or political right can be. But an absurd opinion concerning the king's hereditary right to the crown does not prejudice one that is rational and bottomed upon solid principles of law and policy. If all the absurd theories of lawyers and divines were to vitiate the objects in which they are conversant, we should have no law and no religion left in the world. But an absurd theory on one side of a question forms no justification for alleging a false fact or promulgating mischievous maxims on the other.

THE second claim of the Revolution Society is "a right of cashiering their governors for misconduct". Perhaps the apprehensions our ancestors entertained of forming such a precedent as that "of cashiering for misconduct" was the cause that the declaration of the act, which implied the abdication of King James, was, if it had any fault, rather too guarded and too circumstantial. But all this guard and all this accumulation of circumstances serves to show the spirit of caution which predominated in the national councils in a situation in which men irritated by oppression, and elevated by a triumph over it, are apt to abandon themselves to violent and extreme courses; it shows the anxiety of the great men who influenced the conduct of affairs at that great event to make the Revolution a parent of settlement, and not a nursery of future revolutions.

No government could stand a moment if it could be blown down with anything so loose and indefinite as an opinion of "misconduct". They who led at the Revolution grounded the virtual abdication of King James upon no such light and uncertain principle. They charged him with nothing less than a design, confirmed by a multitude of illegal overt acts, to subvert the Protestant church and state, and their fundamental, unquestionable laws and liberties; they charged him with having broken the original contract between king and people. This was more than misconduct. A grave and overruling necessity obliged them to take the step they took, and took with infinite reluctance, as under that most rigorous of all laws. Their trust for the future preservation of the constitution was not in future revolutions. The grand policy of all their regulations was to render it almost impracticable for any future sovereign to compel the states of the kingdom to have again recourse to those violent remedies. They left the crown what, in the eye and estimation of law, it had ever been- perfectly irresponsible. In order to lighten the crown still further, they aggravated responsibility on ministers of state. By the statute of the 1st of King William, sess. 2nd, called "the act for declaring the rights and liberties of the subject, and for settling the succession of the crown", they enacted that the ministers should serve the crown on the terms of that declaration. They secured soon after the frequent meetings of parliament, by which the whole government would be under the constant inspection and active control of the popular representative and of the magnates of the kingdom. In the next great constitutional act, that of the 12th and 13th of King William, for the further limitation of the crown and better securing the rights and liberties of the subject, they provided "that no pardon under the great seal of England should be pleadable to an impeachment by the Commons in parliament". The rule laid down for government in the Declaration of Right, the constant inspection of parliament, the practical claim of impeachment, they thought infinitely a better security, not only for their constitutional liberty, but against the vices of administration, than the reservation of a right so difficult in the practice, so uncertain in the issue, and often so mischievous in the consequences, as that of "cashiering their governors".

Dr. Price, in this sermon, condemns very properly the practice of gross, adulatory addresses to kings. Instead of this fulsome style, he proposes that his Majesty should be told, on occasions of congratulation, that "he is to consider himself as more properly the servant than the sovereign of his people". For a compliment, this new form of address does not seem to be very soothing. Those who are servants in name, as well as in effect, do not like to be told of their situation, their duty, and their obligations. The slave, in the old play, tells his master, "Haec commemoratio est quasi exprobatio". It is not pleasant as compliment; it is not wholesome as instruction. After all, if the king were to bring himself to echo this new kind of address, to adopt it in terms, and even to take the appellation of Servant of the People as his royal style, how either he or we should be much mended by it I cannot imagine. I have seen very assuming letters, signed "Your most obedient, humble servant". The proudest denomination that ever was endured on earth took a title of still greater humility than that which is now proposed for sovereigns by the Apostle of Liberty. Kings and nations were trampled upon by the foot of one calling himself "the Servant of Servants"; and mandates for deposing sovereigns were sealed with the signet of "the Fisherman".

I should have considered all this as no more than a sort of flippant, vain discourse, in which, as in an unsavory fume, several persons suffer the spirit of liberty to evaporate, if it were not plainly in support of the idea and a part of the scheme of "cashiering kings for misconduct". In that light it is worth some observation.

Kings, in one sense, are undoubtedly the servants of the people because their power has no other rational end than that of the general advantage; but it is not true that they are, in the ordinary sense (by our constitution, at least), anything like servants; the essence of whose situation is to obey the commands of some other and to be removable at pleasure. But the king of Great Britain obeys no other person; all other persons are individually, and collectively too, under him and owe to him a legal obedience. The law, which knows neither to flatter nor to insult, calls this high magistrate not our servant, as this humble divine calls him, but "our sovereign Lord the king"; and we, on our parts, have learned to speak only the primitive language of the law, and not the confused jargon of their Babylonian pulpits.

As he is not to obey us, but as we are to obey the law in him, our constitution has made no sort of provision toward rendering him, as a servant, in any degree responsible. Our constitution knows nothing of a magistrate like the Justicia of Aragon, nor of any court legally appointed, nor of any process legally settled, for submitting the king to the responsibility belonging to all servants. In this he is not distinguished from the Commons and the Lords, who, in their several public capacities, can never be called to an account for their conduct, although the Revolution Society chooses to assert, in direct opposition to one of the wisest and most beautiful parts of our constitution, that "a king is no more than the first servant of the public, created by it, and responsible to it"

Ill would our ancestors at the Revolution have deserved their fame for wisdom if they had found no security for their freedom but in rendering their government feeble in its operations, and precarious in its tenure; if they had been able to contrive no better remedy against arbitrary power than civil confusion. Let these gentlemen state who that representative public is to whom they will affirm the king, as a servant, to be responsible. It will then be time enough for me to produce to them the positive statute law which affirms that he is not.

The ceremony of cashiering kings, of which these gentlemen talk so much at their ease, can rarely, if ever, be performed without force. It then becomes a case of war, and not of constitution. Laws are commanded to hold their tongues amongst arms, and tribunals fall to the ground with the peace they are no longer able to uphold. The Revolution of 1688 was obtained by a just war, in the only case in which any war, and much more a civil war, can be just. Justa bella quibus necessaria. The question of dethroning or, if these gentlemen like the phrase better, "cashiering kings" will always be, as it has always been, an extraordinary question of state, and wholly out of the law — a question (like all other questions of state) of dispositions and of means and of probable consequences rather than of positive rights. As it was not made for common abuses, so it is not to be agitated by common minds. The speculative line of demarcation where obedience ought to end and resistance must begin is faint, obscure, and not easily definable. It is not a single act, or a single event, which determines it. Governments must be abused and deranged, indeed, before it can be thought of; and the prospect of the future must be as bad as the experience of the past. When things are in that lamentable condition, the nature of the disease is to indicate the remedy to those whom nature has qualified to administer in extremities this critical, ambiguous, bitter potion to a distempered state. Times and occasions and provocations will teach their own lessons. The wise will determine from the gravity of the case; the irritable, from sensibility to oppression; the high-minded, from disdain and indignation at abusive power in unworthy hands; the brave and bold, from the love of honorable danger in a generous cause; but, with or without right, a revolution will be the very last resource of the thinking and the good.

THE third head of right, asserted by the pulpit of the Old Jewry, namely, the "right to form a government for ourselves", has, at least, as little countenance from anything done at the Revolution, either in precedent or principle, as the two first of their claims. The Revolution was made to preserve our ancient, indisputable laws and liberties and that ancient constitution of government which is our only security for law and liberty. If you are desirous of knowing the spirit of our constitution and the policy which predominated in that great period which has secured it to this hour, pray look for both in our histories, in our records, in our acts of parliament, and journals of parliament, and not in the sermons of the Old Jewry and the after-dinner toasts of the Revolution Society. In the former you will find other ideas and another language. Such a claim is as ill-suited to our temper and wishes as it is unsupported by any appearance of authority. The very idea of the fabrication of a new government is enough to fill us with disgust and horror. We wished at the period of the Revolution, and do now wish, to derive all we possess as an inheritance from our forefathers. Upon that body and stock of inheritance we have taken care not to inoculate any cyon alien to the nature of the original plant. All the reformations we have hitherto made have proceeded upon the principle of reverence to antiquity; and I hope, nay, I am persuaded, that all those which possibly may be made hereafter will be carefully formed upon analogical precedent, authority, and example.

Our oldest reformation is that of Magna Charta. You will see that Sir Edward Coke, that great oracle of our law, and indeed all the great men who follow him, to Blackstone, are industrious to prove the pedigree of our liberties. They endeavor to prove that the ancient charter, the Magna Charta of King John, was connected with another positive charter from Henry I, and that both the one and the other were nothing more than a reaffirmance of the still more ancient standing law of the kingdom. In the matter of fact, for the greater part these authors appear to be in the right; perhaps not always; but if the lawyers mistake in some particulars, it proves my position still the more strongly, because it demonstrates the powerful prepossession toward antiquity, with which the minds of all our lawyers and legislators, and of all the people whom they wish to influence, have been always filled, and the stationary policy of this kingdom in considering their most sacred rights and franchises as an inheritance.

In the famous law of the 3rd of Charles I, called the Petition of Right, the parliament says to the king, "Your subjects have inherited this freedom", claiming their franchises not on abstract principles "as the rights of men", but as the rights of Englishmen, and as a patrimony derived from their forefathers. Selden and the other profoundly learned men who drew this Petition of Right were as well acquainted, at least, with all the general theories concerning the "rights of men" as any of the discoursers in our pulpits or on your tribune; full as well as Dr. Price or as the Abbe Sieyes. But, for reasons worthy of that practical wisdom which superseded their theoretic science, they preferred this positive, recorded, hereditary title to all which can be dear to the man and the citizen, to that vague speculative right which exposed their sure inheritance to be scrambled for and torn to pieces by every wild, litigious spirit.

The same policy pervades all the laws which have since been made for the preservation of our liberties. In the 1st of William and Mary, in the famous statute called the Declaration of Right, the two Houses utter not a syllable of "a right to frame a government for themselves". You will see that their whole care was to secure the religion, laws, and liberties that had been long possessed, and had been lately endangered. "Taking into their most serious consideration the best means for making such an establishment, that their religion, laws, and liberties might not be in danger of being again subverted", they auspicate all their proceedings by stating as some of those best means, "in the first place" to do "as their ancestors in like cases have usually done for vindicating their ancient rights and liberties, to declare" — and then they pray the king and queen "that it may be declared and enacted that all and singular the rights and liberties asserted and declared are the true ancient and indubitable rights and liberties of the people of this kingdom".

You will observe that from Magna Charta to the Declaration of Right it has been the uniform policy of our constitution to claim and assert our liberties as an entailed inheritance derived to us from our forefathers, and to be transmitted to our posterity — as an estate specially belonging to the people of this kingdom, without any reference whatever to any other more general or prior right. By this means our constitution preserves a unity in so great a diversity of its parts. We have an inheritable crown, an inheritable peerage, and a House of Commons and a people inheriting privileges, franchises, and liberties from a long line of ancestors.

This policy appears to me to be the result of profound reflection, or rather the happy effect of following nature, which is wisdom without reflection, and above it. A spirit of innovation is generally the result of a selfish temper and confined views. People will not look forward to posterity, who never look backward to their ancestors. Besides, the people of England well know that the idea of inheritance furnishes a sure principle of conservation and a sure principle of transmission, without at all excluding a principle of improvement. It leaves acquisition free, but it secures what it acquires. Whatever advantages are obtained by a state proceeding on these maxims are locked fast as in a sort of family settlement, grasped as in a kind of mortmain forever. By a constitutional policy, working after the pattern of nature, we receive, we hold, we transmit our government and our privileges in the same manner in which we enjoy and transmit our property and our lives. The institutions of policy, the goods of fortune, the gifts of providence are handed down to us, and from us, in the same course and order. Our political system is placed in a just correspondence and symmetry with the order of the world and with the mode of existence decreed to a permanent body composed of transitory parts, wherein, by the disposition of a stupendous wisdom, molding together the great mysterious incorporation of the human race, the whole, at one time, is never old or middle-aged or young, but, in a condition of unchangeable constancy, moves on through the varied tenor of perpetual decay, fall, renovation, and progression. Thus, by preserving the method of nature in the conduct of the state, in what we improve we are never wholly new; in what we retain we are never wholly obsolete. By adhering in this manner and on those principles to our forefathers, we are guided not by the superstition of antiquarians, but by the spirit of philosophic analogy. In this choice of inheritance we have given to our frame of polity the image of a relation in blood, binding up the constitution of our country with our dearest domestic ties, adopting our fundamental laws into the bosom of our family affections, keeping inseparable and cherishing with the warmth of all their combined and mutually reflected charities our state, our hearths, our sepulchres, and our altars.

Through the same plan of a conformity to nature in our artificial institutions, and by calling in the aid of her unerring and powerful instincts to fortify the fallible and feeble contrivances of our reason, we have derived several other, and those no small, benefits from considering our liberties in the light of an inheritance. Always acting as if in the presence of canonized forefathers, the spirit of freedom, leading in itself to misrule and excess, is tempered with an awful gravity. This idea of a liberal descent inspires us with a sense of habitual native dignity which prevents that upstart insolence almost inevitably adhering to and disgracing those who are the first acquirers of any distinction. By this means our liberty becomes a noble freedom.

It carries an imposing and majestic aspect. It has a pedigree and illustrating ancestors. It has its bearings and its ensigns armorial. It has its gallery of portraits, its monumental inscriptions, its records, evidences, and titles. We procure reverence to our civil institutions on the principle upon which nature teaches us to revere individual men: on account of their age and on account of those from whom they are descended. All your sophisters cannot produce anything better adapted to preserve a rational and manly freedom than the course that we have pursued, who have chosen our nature rather than our speculations, our breasts rather than our inventions, for the great conservatories and magazines of our rights and privileges.

YOU MIGHT, IF YOU PLEASED, have profited of our example and have given to your recovered freedom a correspondent dignity. Your privileges, though discontinued, were not lost to memory. Your constitution, it is true, whilst you were out of possession, suffered waste and dilapidation; but you possessed in some parts the walls and in all the foundations of a noble and venerable castle. You might have repaired those walls; you might have built on those old foundations. Your constitution was suspended before it was perfected, but you had the elements of a constitution very nearly as good as could be wished. In your old states you possessed that variety of parts corresponding with the various descriptions of which your community was happily composed; you had all that combination and all that opposition of interests; you had that action and counteraction which, in the natural and in the political world, from the reciprocal struggle of discordant powers, draws out the harmony of the universe. These opposed and conflicting interests which you considered as so great a blemish in your old and in our present constitution interpose a salutary check to all precipitate resolutions. They render deliberation a matter, not of choice, but of necessity; they make all change a subject of compromise, which naturally begets moderation; they produce temperaments preventing the sore evil of harsh, crude, unqualified reformations, and rendering all the headlong exertions of arbitrary power, in the few or in the many, forever impracticable. Through that diversity of members and interests, general liberty had as many securities as there were separate views in the several orders, whilst, by pressing down the whole by the weight of a real monarchy, the separate parts would have been prevented from warping and starting from their allotted places.

You had all these advantages in your ancient states, but you chose to act as if you had never been molded into civil society and had everything to begin anew. You began ill, because you began by despising everything that belonged to you. You set up your trade without a capital. If the last generations of your country appeared without much luster in your eyes, you might have passed them by and derived your claims from a more early race of ancestors. Under a pious predilection for those ancestors, your imaginations would have realized in them a standard of virtue and wisdom beyond the vulgar practice of the hour; and you would have risen with the example to whose imitation you aspired. Respecting your forefathers, you would have been taught to respect yourselves. You would not have chosen to consider the French as a people of yesterday, as a nation of lowborn servile wretches until the emancipating year of 1789. In order to furnish, at the expense of your honor, an excuse to your apologists here for several enormities of yours, you would not have been content to be represented as a gang of Maroon slaves suddenly broke loose from the house of bondage, and therefore to be pardoned for your abuse of the liberty to which you were not accustomed and ill fitted. Would it not, my worthy friend, have been wiser to have you thought, what I, for one, always thought you, a generous and gallant nation, long misled to your disadvantage by your high and romantic sentiments of fidelity, honor, and loyalty; that events had been unfavorable to you, but that you were not enslaved through any illiberal or servile disposition; that in your most devoted submission you were actuated by a principle of public spirit, and that it was your country you worshiped in the person of your king? Had you made it to be understood that in the delusion of this amiable error you had gone further than your wise ancestors, that you were resolved to resume your ancient privileges, whilst you preserved the spirit of your ancient and your recent loyalty and honor; or if, diffident of yourselves and not clearly discerning the almost obliterated constitution of your ancestors, you had looked to your neighbors in this land who had kept alive the ancient principles and models of the old common law of Europe meliorated and adapted to its present state — by following wise examples you would have given new examples of wisdom to the world. You would have rendered the cause of liberty venerable in the eyes of every worthy mind in every nation. You would have shamed despotism from the earth by showing that freedom was not only reconcilable, but, as when well disciplined it is, auxiliary to law. You would have had an unoppressive but a productive revenue. You would have had a flourishing commerce to feed it. You would have had a free constitution, a potent monarchy, a disciplined army, a reformed and venerated clergy, a mitigated but spirited nobility to lead your virtue, not to overlay it; you would have had a liberal order of commons to emulate and to recruit that nobility; you would have had a protected, satisfied, laborious, and obedient people, taught to seek and to recognize the happiness that is to be found by virtue in all conditions; in which consists the true moral equality of mankind, and not in that monstrous fiction which, by inspiring false ideas and vain expectations into men destined to travel in the obscure walk of laborious life, serves only to aggravate and embitter that real inequality which it never can remove, and which the order of civil life establishes as much for the benefit of those whom it must leave in a humble state as those whom it is able to exalt to a condition more splendid, but not more happy. You had a smooth and easy career of felicity and glory laid open to you, beyond anything recorded in the history of the world, but you have shown that difficulty is good for man.

Middle-Aged Perspective

Thomas Paine (1737-1809)

Rights of Man (1791)

Arthur Young (1741-1820)

The Example of France, a Warning to Britain (1793)

Rights of Man (1791)

Thomas Paine (1737-1809)

Rights of Man

Among the incivilities by which nations or individuals provoke and irritate each other, Mr. Burke's pamphlet on the French Revolution is an extraordinary instance. Neither the People of France, nor the National Assembly, were troubling themselves about the affairs of England, or the English Parliament; and that Mr. Burke should commence an unprovoked attack upon them, both in Parliament and in public, is a conduct that cannot be pardoned on the score of manners, nor justified on that of policy. There is scarcely an epithet of abuse to be found in the English language, with which Mr. Burke has not loaded the French Nation and the National Assembly. Everything which rancour, prejudice, ignorance or knowledge could suggest, is poured forth in the copious fury of near four hundred pages. In the strain and on the plan Mr. Burke was writing, he might have written on to as many thousands. When the tongue or the pen is let loose in a frenzy of passion, it is the man, and not the subject, that becomes exhausted. Hitherto Mr. Burke has been mistaken and disappointed in the opinions he had formed of the affairs of France; but such is the ingenuity of his hope, or the malignancy of his despair, that it furnishes him with new pretences to go on. There was a time when it was impossible to make Mr. Burke believe there would be any Revolution in France. His opinion then was, that the French had neither spirit to undertake it nor fortitude to support it; and now that there is one, he seeks an escape by condemning it. Not sufficiently content with abusing the National Assembly, a great part of his work is taken up with abusing Dr. Price (one of the best-hearted men that lives) and the two societies in England known by the name of the Revolution Society and the Society for Constitutional Information. Dr. Price had preached a sermon on the 4th of November, 1789, being the anniversary of what is called in England the Revolution, which took place 1688. Mr. Burke, speaking of this sermon, says: "The political Divine proceeds dogmatically to assert, that by the principles of the Revolution, the people of England have acquired three fundamental rights:

1. To choose our own governors.
2. To cashier them for misconduct.
3. To frame a government for ourselves."

Dr. Price does not say that the right to do these things exists in this or in that person, or in this or in that description of persons, but that it exists in the whole; that it is a right resident in the nation. Mr. Burke, on the contrary, denies that such a right exists in the nation, either in whole or in part, or that it exists anywhere; and, what is still more strange and marvellous, he says: "that the people of England utterly disclaim such a right, and that they will resist the practical assertion of it with their lives and fortunes." That men should take up arms and spend their lives and fortunes, not to maintain their rights, but to maintain they have not rights, is an entirely new species of discovery, and suited to the paradoxical genius of Mr. Burke. The method which Mr. Burke takes to prove that the people of England have no such rights, and that such rights do not now exist in the nation, either in whole or in part, or anywhere at all, is of the same marvellous and monstrous kind with what he has already said; for his arguments are that the persons, or the generation of persons, in whom they did exist, are dead, and with them the right is dead also. To prove this, he quotes a declaration made by Parliament about a hundred years ago, to William and Mary, in these words: "The Lords Spiritual and Temporal, and Commons, do, in the name of the people aforesaid" (meaning the people of England then living) "most humbly and faithfully submit themselves, their heirs and posterities, for EVER." He quotes a clause of another Act of Parliament made in the same reign, the terms of which he says, "bind us" (meaning the people of their day), "our heirs and our posterity, to them, their heirs and posterity, to the end of time." Mr. Burke conceives his point sufficiently established by producing those clauses, which he enforces by saying that they exclude the right of the nation for ever. And not yet content with making such declarations, repeated over and over again, he farther says, "that if the people of England possessed such a right before the Revolution" (which he acknowledges to have been the case, not only in England, but throughout Europe, at an early period), "yet that the English Nation did, at the time of the Revolution, most solemnly renounce and abdicate it, for themselves, and for all their posterity, forever." As Mr. Burke occasionally applies the poison drawn from his horrid principles, not only to the English nation, but to the French Revolution and the National Assembly, and charges that august, illuminated and illuminating body of men with the epithet of usurpers, I shall, sans ceremonie, place another system of principles in opposition to his.

     The English Parliament of 1688 did a certain thing, which, for themselves and their constituents, they had a right to do, and which it appeared right should be done. But, in addition to this right, which they possessed by delegation, they set up another right by assumption, that of binding and controlling posterity to the end of time. The case, therefore, divides itself into two parts; the right which they possessed by delegation, and the right which they set up by assumption. The first is admitted; but with respect to the second, I reply There never did, there never will, and there never can, exist a Parliament, or any description of men, or any generation of men, in any country, possessed of the right or the power of binding and controlling posterity to the "end of time," or of commanding for ever how the world shall be governed, or who shall govern it; and therefore all such clauses, acts or declarations by which the makers of them attempt to do what they have neither the right nor the power to do, nor the power to execute, are in themselves null and void. Every age and generation must be as free to act for itself in all cases as the age and generations which preceded it. The vanity and presumption of governing beyond the grave is the most ridiculous and insolent of all tyrannies. Man has no property in man; neither has any generation a property in the generations which are to follow. The Parliament or the people of 1688, or of any other period, had no more right to dispose of the people of the present day, or to bind or to control them in any shape whatever, than the parliament or the people of the present day have to dispose of, bind or control those who are to live a hundred or a thousand years hence. Every generation is, and must be, competent to all the purposes which its occasions require. It is the living, and not the dead, that are to be accommodated. When man ceases to be, his power and his wants cease with him; and having no longer any participation in the concerns of this world, he has no longer any authority in directing who shall be its governors, or how its government shall be organised, or how administered. I am not contending for nor against any form of government, nor for nor against any party, here or elsewhere. That which a whole nation chooses to do it has a right to do. Mr. Burke says, No. Where, then, does the right exist? I am contending for the rights of the living, and against their being willed away and controlled and contracted for by the manuscript assumed authority of the dead, and Mr. Burke is contending for the authority of the dead over the rights and freedom of the living. There was a time when kings disposed of their crowns by will upon their death-beds, and consigned the people, like beasts of the field, to whatever successor they appointed. This is now so exploded as scarcely to be remembered, and so monstrous as hardly to be believed. But the Parliamentary clauses upon which Mr. Burke builds his political church are of the same nature. The laws of every country must be analogous to some common principle. In England no parent or master, nor all the authority of Parliament, omnipotent as it has called itself, can bind or control the personal freedom even of an individual beyond the age of twenty-one years. On what ground of right, then, could the Parliament of 1688, or any other Parliament, bind all posterity forever? Those who have quitted the world, and those who have not yet arrived at it, are as remote from each other as the utmost stretch of mortal imagination can conceive. What possible obligation, then, can exist between them- what rule or principle can be laid down that of two nonentities, the one out of existence and the other not in, and who never can meet in this world, the one should control the other to the end of time? In England it is said that money cannot be taken out of the pockets of the people without their consent. But who authorised, or who could authorise, the Parliament of 1688 to control and take away the freedom of posterity (who were not in existence to give or to withhold their consent) and limit and confine their right of acting in certain cases forever? A greater absurdity cannot present itself to the understanding of man than what Mr. Burke offers to his readers. He tells them, and he tells the world to come, that a certain body of men who existed a hundred years ago made a law, and that there does not exist in the nation, nor ever will, nor ever can, a power to alter it. Under how many subtilties or absurdities has the divine right to govern been imposed on the credulity of mankind? Mr. Burke has discovered a new one, and he has shortened his journey to Rome by appealing to the power of this infallible Parliament of former days, and he produces what it has done as of divine authority, for that power must certainly be more than human which no human power to the end of time can alter. But Mr. Burke has done some service- not to his cause, but to his country- by bringing those clauses into public view. They serve to demonstrate how necessary it is at all times to watch against the attempted encroachment of power, and to prevent its running to excess. It is somewhat extraordinary that the offence for which James II. was expelled, that of setting up power by assumption, should be reacted, under another shape and form, by the Parliament that expelled him. It shows that the Rights of Man were but imperfectly understood at the Revolution, for certain it is that the right which that Parliament set up by assumption (for by the delegation it had not, and could not have it, because none could give it) over the persons and freedom of posterity for ever was of the same tyrannical unfounded kind which James attempted to set up over the Parliament and the nation, and for which he was expelled. The only difference is (for in principle they differ not) that the one was an usurper over living, and the other over the unborn; and as the one has no better authority to stand upon than the other, both of them must be equally null and void, and of no effect. From what, or from whence, does Mr. Burke prove the right of any human power to bind posterity forever? He has produced his clauses, but he must produce also his proofs that such a right existed, and show how it existed. If it ever existed it must now exist, for whatever appertains to the nature of man cannot be annihilated by man. It is the nature of man to die, and he will continue to die as long as he continues to be born. But Mr. Burke has set up a sort of political Adam, in whom all posterity are bound for ever. He must, therefore, prove that his Adam possessed such a power, or such a right. The weaker any cord is, the less will it bear to be stretched, and the worse is the policy to stretch it, unless it is intended to break it. Had anyone proposed the overthrow of Mr. Burke's positions, he would have proceeded as Mr. Burke has done. He would have magnified the authorities, on purpose to have called the right of them into question; and the instant the question of right was started, the authorities must have been given up. It requires but a very small glance of thought to perceive that although laws made in one generation often continue in force through succeeding generations, yet they continue to derive their force from the consent of the living. A law not repealed continues in force, not because it cannot be repealed, but because it is not repealed; and the non-repealing passes for consent. But Mr. Burke's clauses have not even this qualification in their favour. They become null, by attempting to become immortal. The nature of them precludes consent. They destroy the right which they might have, by grounding it on a right which they cannot have. Immortal power is not a human right, and therefore cannot be a right of Parliament. The Parliament of 1688 might as well have passed an act to have authorised themselves to live forever, as to make their authority live forever. All, therefore, that can be said of those clauses is that they are a formality of words, of as much import as if those who used them had addressed a congratulation to themselves, and in the oriental style of antiquity had said: O Parliament, live forever! The circumstances of the world are continually changing, and the opinions of men change also; and as government is for the living, and not for the dead, it is the living only that has any right in it. That which may be thought right and found convenient in one age may be thought wrong and found inconvenient in another. In such cases, who is to decide, the living or the dead? As almost one hundred pages of Mr. Burke's book are employed upon these clauses, it will consequently follow that if the clauses themselves, so far as they set up an assumed usurped dominion over posterity forever, are unauthoritative, and in their nature null and void; that all his voluminous inferences, and declamation drawn therefrom, or founded thereon, are null and void also; and on this ground I rest the matter. We now come more particularly to the affairs of France. Mr. Burke's book has the appearance of being written as instruction to the French nation; but if I may permit myself the use of an extravagant metaphor, suited to the extravagance of the case, it is darkness attempting to illuminate light. While I am writing this there are accidentally before me some proposals for a declaration of rights by the Marquis de la Fayette (I ask his pardon for using his former address, and do it only for distinction's sake) to the National Assembly, on the 11th of July, 1789, three days before the taking of the Bastille, and I cannot but remark with astonishment how opposite the sources are from which that gentleman and Mr. Burke draw their principles. Instead of referring to musty records and mouldy parchments to prove that the rights of the living are lost, "renounced and abdicated forever," by those who are now no more, as Mr. Burke has done, M. de la Fayette applies to the living world, and emphatically says: "Call to mind the sentiments which nature has engraved on the heart of every citizen, and which take a new force when they are solemnly recognised by all:- For a nation to love liberty, it is sufficient that she knows it; and to be free, it is sufficient that she wills it." How dry, barren, and obscure is the source from which Mr. Burke labors! and how ineffectual, though gay with flowers, are all his declamation and his arguments compared with these clear, concise, and soul-animating sentiments! Few and short as they are, they lead on to a vast field of generous and manly thinking, and do not finish, like Mr. Burke's periods, with music in the ear, and nothing in the heart. As I have introduced M. de la Fayette, I will take the liberty of adding an anecdote respecting his farewell address to the Congress of America in 1783, and which occurred fresh to my mind, when I saw Mr. Burke's thundering attack on the French Revolution. M. de la Fayette went to America at the early period of the war, and continued a volunteer in her service to the end. His conduct through the whole of that enterprise is one of the most extraordinary that is to be found in the history of a young man, scarcely twenty years of age. Situated in a country that was like the lap of sensual pleasure, and with the means of enjoying it, how few are there to be found who would exchange such a scene for the woods and wildernesses of America, and pass the flowery years of youth in unprofitable danger and hardship! but such is the fact. When the war ended, and he was on the point of taking his final departure, he presented himself to Congress, and contemplating in his affectionate farewell the Revolution he had seen, expressed himself in these words: "May this great monument raised to liberty serve as a lesson to the oppressor, and an example to the oppressed!" When this address came to the hands of Dr. Franklin, who was then in France, he applied to Count Vergennes to have it inserted in the French Gazette, but never could obtain his consent. The fact was that Count Vergennes was an aristocratical despot at home, and dreaded the example of the American Revolution in France, as certain other persons now dread the example of the French Revolution in England, and Mr. Burke's tribute of fear (for in this light his book must be considered) runs parallel with Count Vergennes' refusal. But to return more particularly to his work. "We have seen," says Mr. Burke, "the French rebel against a mild and lawful monarch, with more fury, outrage, and insult, than any people has been known to rise against the most illegal usurper, or the most sanguinary tyrant." This is one among a thousand other instances, in which Mr. Burke shows that he is ignorant of the springs and principles of the French Revolution. It was not against Louis XVI. but against the despotic principles of the Government, that the nation revolted. These principles had not their origin in him, but in the original establishment, many centuries back: and they were become too deeply rooted to be removed, and the Augean stables of parasites and plunderers too abominably filthy to be cleansed by anything short of a complete and universal Revolution. When it becomes necessary to do anything, the whole heart and soul should go into the measure, or not attempt it. That crisis was then arrived, and there remained no choice but to act with determined vigor, or not to act at all. The king was known to be the friend of the nation, and this circumstance was favorable to the enterprise. Perhaps no man bred up in the style of an absolute king, ever possessed a heart so little disposed to the exercise of that species of power as the present King of France. But the principles of the Government itself still remained the same. The Monarch and the Monarchy were distinct and separate things; and it was against the established despotism of the latter, and not against the person or principles of the former, that the revolt commenced, and the Revolution has been carried. Mr. Burke does not attend to the distinction between men and principles, and, therefore, he does not see that a revolt may take place against the despotism of the latter, while there lies no charge of despotism against the former. The natural moderation of Louis XVI. contributed nothing to alter the hereditary despotism of the monarchy. All the tyrannies of former reigns, acted under that hereditary despotism, were still liable to be revived in the hands of a successor. It was not the respite of a reign that would satisfy France, enlightened as she was then become. A casual discontinuance of the practice of despotism, is not a discontinuance of its principles: the former depends on the virtue of the individual who is in immediate possession of the power; the latter, on the virtue and fortitude of the nation. In the case of Charles I. and James II. of England, the revolt was against the personal despotism of the men; whereas in France, it was against the hereditary despotism of the established Government. But men who can consign over the rights of posterity for ever on the authority of a mouldy parchment, like Mr. Burke, are not qualified to judge of this Revolution. It takes in a field too vast for their views to explore, and proceeds with a mightiness of reason they cannot keep pace with. But there are many points of view in which this

Revolution may be considered. When despotism has established itself for ages in a country, as in France, it is not in the person of the king only that it resides. It has the appearance of being so in show, and in nominal authority; but it is not so in practice and in fact. It has its standard everywhere. Every office and department has its despotism, founded upon custom and usage. Every place has its Bastille, and every Bastille its despot. The original hereditary despotism resident in the person of the king, divides and sub-divides itself into a thousand shapes and forms, till at last the whole of it is acted by deputation. This was the case in France; and against this species of despotism, proceeding on through an endless labyrinth of office till the source of it is scarcely perceptible, there is no mode of redress. It strengthens itself by assuming the appearance of duty, and tyrannies under the pretence of obeying. When a man reflects on the condition which France was in from the nature of her government, he will see other causes for revolt than those which immediately connect themselves with the person or character of Louis XVI. There were, if I may so express it, a thousand despotisms to be reformed in France, which had grown up under the hereditary despotism of the monarchy, and became so rooted as to be in a great measure independent of it. Between the Monarchy, the Parliament, and the Church there was a rivalship of despotism; besides the feudal despotism operating locally, and the ministerial despotism operating everywhere. But Mr. Burke, by considering the king as the only possible object of a revolt, speaks as if France was a village, in which everything that passed must be known to its commanding officer, and no oppression could be acted but what he could immediately control. Mr. Burke might have been in the Bastille his whole life, as well under Louis XVI. as Louis XIV., and neither the one nor the other have known that such a man as Burke existed. The despotic principles of the government were the same in both reigns, though the dispositions of the men were as remote as tyranny and benevolence. What Mr. Burke considers as a reproach to the French Revolution (that of bringing it forward under a reign more mild than the preceding ones) is one of its highest honors. The Revolutions that have taken place in other European countries, have been excited by personal hatred. The rage was against the man, and he became the victim. But, in the instance of France we see a Revolution generated in the rational contemplation of the Rights of Man, and distinguishing from the beginning between persons and principles. But Mr. Burke appears to have no idea of principles when he is contemplating Governments. "Ten years ago," says he, "I could have felicitated France on her having a Government, without inquiring what the nature of that Government was, or how it was administered." Is this the language of a rational man? Is it the language of a heart feeling as it ought to feel for the rights and happiness of the human race? On this ground, Mr. Burke must compliment all the Governments in the world, while the victims who suffer under them, whether sold into slavery, or tortured out of existence, are wholly forgotten. It is power, and not principles, that Mr. Burke venerates; and under this abominable depravity he is disqualified to judge between them. Thus much for his opinion as to the occasions of the French Revolution. I now proceed to other considerations. I know a place in America called Point-no-Point, because as you proceed along the shore, gay and flowery as Mr. Burke's language, it continually recedes and presents itself at a distance before you; but when you have got as far as you can go, there is no point at all. Just thus it is with Mr. Burke's three hundred and sixty-six pages. It is therefore difficult to reply to him. But as the points he wishes to establish may be inferred from what he abuses, it is in his paradoxes that we must look for his arguments. As to the tragic paintings by which Mr. Burke has outraged his own imagination, and seeks to work upon that of his readers, they are very well calculated for theatrical representation, where facts are manufactured for the sake of show, and accommodated to produce, through the weakness of sympathy, a weeping effect. But Mr. Burke should recollect that he is writing history, and not plays, and that his readers will expect truth, and not the spouting rant of high-toned exclamation. When we see a man dramatically lamenting in a publication intended to be believed that "The age of chivalry is gone! that The glory of Europe is extinguished forever! that The unbought grace of life (if anyone knows what it is), the cheap defence of nations, the nurse of manly sentiment and heroic enterprise is gone!" and all this because the Quixot age of chivalry nonsense is gone, what opinion can we form of his judgment, or what regard can we pay to his facts? In the rhapsody of his imagination he has discovered a world of wind mills, and his sorrows are that there are no Quixots to attack them. But if the age of aristocracy, like that of chivalry, should fall (and they had originally some connection) Mr. Burke, the trumpeter of the Order, may continue his parody to the end, and finish with exclaiming: "Othello's occupation's gone!" Notwithstanding Mr. Burke's horrid paintings, when the French Revolution is compared with the Revolutions of other countries, the astonishment will be that it is marked with so few sacrifices; but this astonishment will cease when we reflect that principles, and not persons, were the meditated objects of destruction. The mind of the nation was acted upon by a higher stimulus than what the consideration of persons could inspire, and sought a higher conquest than could be produced by the downfall of an enemy.

Among the few who fell there do not appear to be any that were intentionally singled out. They all of them had their fate in the circumstances of the moment, and were not pursued with that long, cold-blooded unabated revenge which pursued the unfortunate Scotch in the affair of 1745. Through the whole of Mr. Burke's book I do not observe that the Bastille is mentioned more than once, and that with a kind of implication as if he were sorry it was pulled down, and wished it were built up again. "We have rebuilt Newgate," says he, "and tenanted the mansion; and we have prisons almost as strong as the Bastille for those who dare to libel the queens of France." As to what a madman like the person called Lord George Gordon might say, and to whom Newgate is rather a bedlam than a prison, it is unworthy a rational consideration. It was a madman that libelled, and that is sufficient apology; and it afforded an opportunity for confining him, which was the thing that was wished for. But certain it is that Mr. Burke, who does not call himself a madman (whatever other people may do), has libelled in the most unprovoked manner, and in the grossest style of the most vulgar abuse, the whole representative authority of France, and yet Mr. Burke takes his seat in the British House of Commons! From his violence and his grief, his silence on some points and his excess on others, it is difficult not to believe that Mr. Burke is sorry, extremely sorry, that arbitrary power, the power of the Pope and the Bastille, are pulled down. Not one glance of compassion, not one commiserating reflection that I can find throughout his book, has he bestowed on those who lingered out the most wretched of lives, a life without hope in the most miserable of prisons. It is painful to behold a man employing his talents to corrupt himself. Nature has been kinder to Mr. Burke than he is to her. He is not affected by the reality of distress touching his heart, but by the showy resemblance of it striking his imagination. He pities the plumage, but forgets the dying bird. Accustomed to kiss the aristocratical hand that hath purloined him from himself, he degenerates into a composition of art, and the genuine soul of nature forsakes him. His hero or his heroine must be a tragedy- victim expiring in show, and not the real prisoner of misery, sliding into death in the silence of a dungeon. As Mr. Burke has passed over the whole transaction of the Bastille (and his silence is nothing in his favour), and has entertained his readers with reflections on supposed facts distorted into real falsehoods, I will give, since he has not, some account of the circumstances which preceded that transaction. They will serve to show that less mischief could scarcely have accompanied such an event when considered with the treacherous and hostile aggravations of the enemies of the Revolution. The mind can hardly picture to itself a more tremendous scene than what the city of Paris exhibited at the time of taking the Bastille, and for two days before and after, nor perceive the possibility of its quieting so soon. At a distance this transaction has appeared only as an act of heroism standing on itself, and the close political connection it had with the Revolution is lost in the brilliancy of the achievement. But we are to consider it as the strength of the parties brought man to man, and contending for the issue. The Bastille was to be either the prize or the prison of the assailants. The downfall of it included the idea of the downfall of despotism, and this compounded image was become as figuratively united as Bunyan's Doubting Castle and Giant Despair.

The Example of France, a Warning to Britain (1793)

Arthur Young (1741-1820)

ON THE REVOLUTION OF FRANCE.

THE gross infamy which attended lettres de cachet and the Bastile, during the whole reign of Louis XV. made them esteemed in England, by people not well informed, as the most prominent features of the despotism of France. They were certainly carried to an access hardly credible; to the length of being sold, with blanks, to be filled up with names at the pleasure of the purchaser; who was thus able, in the gratification of private revenge, to tear a man from the bosom of his family, and bury him in a dungeon, where he would exist forgotten, and die unknown!1—But such excesses could not be common in any country; and they were reduced almost to nothing, from the accession of the present King. The great mass of the people, by which I mean the lower and middle ranks, could suffer very little from such engines, and as few of them are objects of jealousy, had there been nothing else to complain of, it is not probable they would ever have been brought to take arms. The abuses attending the levy of taxes were heavy and universal. The kingdom was parcelled into generalities, with an intendant at the head of each, into whose hands the whole power of the crown was delegated for every thing except the military authority; but particularly for all affairs of finance. The generalities were subdivided into elections, at the head of which was a sub-de-legué, appointed by the intendant. The rolls of the taille, capitation, vingtiêmes, and other taxes, were distributed among districts, parishes, and individuals, at the pleasure of the intendant, who could exempt, change, add, or diminish, at pleasure. Such an enormous power, constantly acting, and from which no man was free, might in the nature of things, degenerate in many cases into absolute tyranny. It must be obvious, that the friends, acquaintances, and dependents of the intendant, and of all hissub-delegués,and the friends of these friends, to a long chain of dependence, might be favoured in taxation at the expence of their miserable neighbours; and that noblemen, in favour at court, to whose protection the intendant himself would naturally look up, could find little difficulty in throwing much of the weight of their taxes on others, without a similar support. Instances, and even gross ones, have been reported to me in many parts of the kingdom, that made me shudder at the oppression to which numbers must have been condemned, by the undue favours granted to such crooked influence. But, without recurring to such cases, what must have been the state of the poor people paying heavy taxes, from which the nobility and clergy were exempted? A cruel aggravation of their misery, to see those who could best afford to pay, exempted because able! —The inrolments for the militia, which the cahiers call an injustice without example,2were another dreadful scourge on the peasantry; and, as married men were exempted from it, occasioned in some degree that mischievous population, which brought beings into the world, in order for little else than to be starved. The corvées, or police of the roads, were annually the ruin of many hundreds of farmers; more than 300 were reduced to beggary in filling up one vale in Loraine: all these oppressions fell on the tiers étatonly; the nobility and clergy having been equally exempted from tailles, militia, and corvées. The penal code of finance makes one shudder at the horrors of punishment inadequate to the crime. A few features will sufficiently characterize the old government of France.

1. Smugglers of salt, armed and assembled to the number of five, in Provence, a fine of500 liv. and nine years gallies; —in all the rest of the kingdom, death.
2. Smugglers armed, assembled, but in number under five, a fine of300 liv. and three years gallies. Second offence, death.
3. Smugglers, without arms, but with horses, carts, or boats; a fine of300 liv.if not paid, three years gallies. Second offence, 400 liv. and nine years gallies.—In Dauphiné, second offence, gallies for life. In Provence, five years gallies.
4. Smugglers, who carry the salt on their backs, and without arms, a fine of200 liv. and, if not paid, are flogged and branded. Second offence, a fine of300 liv. and six years gallies.

5. Women, married and single, smugglers, first offence, a fine of100 liv. Second, 300 liv. Third, flogged, and banished the kingdom for life. Husbands responsible both in fine and body.
6. Children smugglers, the same as women.—Fathers and mothers responsible; and for defect of payment flogged.
7. Nobles, if smugglers, deprived of their nobility; and their houses rased to the ground.
8. Any persons in employment (I suppose in the salt works or the revenue), if smugglers, death. And such as assist in the theft of salt in the transport, hanged.
9. Soldiers smuggling, with arms, are hanged; without arms, gallies for life.
10. Buying smuggled salt to resell it, the same punishments as for smuggling.
11. Persons in the salt employments, empowered if two, or one with two witnesses, to enter and examine houses even of the privileged orders.
12. All families, and persons liable to the taille, in the provinces of the Grandes Gabelles in rolled, and their consumption of salt for the pot and saliére (that is the daily consumption, exclusive of salting meat, &c. &c.) estimated at 7lb. a head per annum, which quantity they are forced to buy whether they want it or not, under the pain of various fines according to the case.

  The Capitaineries were a dreadful scourge on all the occupiers of land. By this term, is to be understood the paramountship of certain districts, granted by the king, to princes of the blood, by which they were put in possession of the property of all game, even on lands not belonging to them; and, what is very singular, on manors granted long before to individuals; so that the erecting of a district into a capitainerie, was an annihilation of all manorial rights to game within it. This was a trifling business, in comparison to other circumstances; for, in speaking of the preservation of the game in these capitaineries it must be observed, that by game it must be understood whole droves of wild boars, and herds of deer not confined by any wall or pale, but wandering, at pleasure, over the whole country, to the destruction of crops; and to the peopling of the gallies by the wretched peasants, who presumed to kill them, in order to save that food which was to support their helpless children. The game in the capitainerie of Montceau, in four parishes only, did mischief to the amount of 184,263 liv. per annum.4No wonder then that we should find the people asking, "Nous demandons à grand cris la destruction des capitaineries & celle de toute sorte de gibier."5And what are we to think of demanding, as a favour, the permission—"De nettoyer ses grains, de faucher les prés artificiels, & d'enlever ses chaumes sans égard pour la perdrix on tout autre gibier." Now, an English reader will scarcely understand it without being told, that there were numerous edicts for preserving the game which prohibited weeding and hoeing, lest the young partridges should be disturbed; steeping seed, lest it should injure the game; manuring with night soil, lest the flavour of the partridges should be injured by feeding on the corn so produced; mowing hay, &c. before a certain time, so late as to spoil many crops; and taking away the stubble, which would deprive the birds of shelter. The tyranny exercised in thesecapitaineries, which extended over 400 leagues of country, was so great, that many cahiers demanded the utter suppression of them. Such were the exertions of arbitrary power which the lower orders felt directly from the royal authority; but, heavy as they were, it is a question whether the others, suffered circuitously through the nobility and the clergy, were not yet more oppressive? Nothing can exceed the complaints made in the cahiers under this head. They speak of the dispensation of justice in the manorial courts, as comprizing every species of despotism: the districts indeterminate—appeals endless—irreconcileable to liberty and prosperity—and irrevocably proscribed in the opinion of the public —augmenting litigations—favouring every species of chicane—ruining the parties—not only by enormous expences on the most petty objects, but by a dreadful loss of time. The judges commonly ignorant pretenders, who hold their courts in cabarets, and are absolutely dependent on the seigneurs, in consequence of their feudal powers. They are "vexations qui sont le plus grand fléau des peuples.9 —Esclavage affligeant10—Ce régime desastreuse.1111a—That the feodalitébe for ever abolished. The countryman is tyrannically enslaved by it. Fixed and heavy rents; vexatious processes to secure them; appreciated unjustly to augment: rents, solidaires, and revenchables; rents,chéantes,and levantes, fumages. Fines at every change of the property, in the direct as well as collateral line; feudal redemption (retraite); fines on sale, to the 8th and even the 6th penny; redemptions (rachats) injurious in their origin, and still more so in their extension; banalité of the mill,12of the oven, and of the wine and cyder-press; corveésby custom; corveésby usage of the fief; corveés established by unjust decrees; corveésarbitrary, and even phantastical; servitudes; prestations, extravagant and burthensome: collections by assessments incollectible; aveux, minus, impunissemens; litigations ruinous and without end: the rod of seigneural finance for ever shaken over our heads; vexation, ruin, outrage, violence, and destructive servitude, under which the peasants, almost on a level with Polish slaves, can never but be miserable, vile, and oppressed.13They demand also, that the use of hand-mills be free; and hope that posterity if possible, may be ignorant that feudal tyranny in Bretagne, armed with the judicial power, has not blushed even in these times, at breaking hand-mills, and at selling annually to the miserable, the faculty of bruising between two stones a measure of buck-wheat or barley.14The very terms of these complaints are unknown in England, and consequently untranslatable: they have probably arisen long since the feudal system ceased in this kingdom. What are these tortures of the peasantry in Bretagne, which they call chevauchés,15quintaines, soule, saut de poisson, baiser de marieés;16chansons; transporte d'œuf sur un charette; silence des grenouilles;17corvée à misericorde; milods; leide; couponage; cartelage; barage;18fouage;19marechaussé; banvin;20ban d'aôut; trousses; gelinage; civerage; taillabilité; vingtain;21sterlage; bordelage;22minage;23ban de vendanges; droit d'accapte.24In passing through many of the

French provinces, I was struck with the various and heavy complaints of the farmers and little proprietors of the feudal grievances, with the weight of which their industry was burthened; but I could not then conceive the multiplicity of the shackles which kept them poor and depressed. I understood it better afterwards, from the conversation and complaints of some grand seigneurs, as the revolution advanced; and I then learned, that the principal rental of many estates consisted in services and feudal tenures; by the baneful influence of which the industry of the people was almost exterminated. In regard to the oppressions of the clergy, as to tythes, I must do that body a justice, to which a claim cannot be laid in England. Though the ecclesiastical tenth was levied in France more severely than usual in Italy, yet was it never exacted with such horrid greediness as is at present the disgrace of England. When taken in kind, no such thing was known in any part of France, where I made inquiries, as a tenth; it was always a twelfth, or a thirteenth, or even a twentieth of the produce. And in no part of the kingdom did a new article of culture pay anything; thus turnips, cabbages, clover, chicorée, potatoes, &c. &c. paid nothing. In many parts, meadows were exempted. Silk worms nothing. Olives in some places paid—in more they did not. Cows nothing. Lambs from the 12th to the 21st. Wool nothing.—Such mildness, in the levy of this odious tax, is absolutely unknown in England. But mild as it was, the burthen to people groaning under so many other oppressions, united to render their situation so bad that no change could be for the worse. But these were not all the evils with which the people struggled. The administration of justice was partial, venal, infamous. I have, in conversation with many very sensible men, in different parts of the kingdom, met with something of content with their government, in all other respects than this; but upon the question of expecting justice to be really and fairly administered, every one confessed there was no such thing to be looked for. The conduct of the parliaments was profligate and atrocious. Upon almost every cause that came before them, interest was openly made with the judges: and woe betided the man who, with a cause to support, had no means of conciliating favour, either by the beauty of a handsome wife, or by other methods. It has been said, by many writers, that property was as secure under the old government of France as it is in England; and the assertion might possibly be true, as far as any violence from the King, his ministers, or the great was concerned: but for all that mass of property, which comes in every country to be litigated in courts of justice, there was not even the shadow of security, unless the parties were totally and equally unknown, and totally and equally honest; in every other case, he who had the best interest with the judges, was sure to be the winner. To reflecting minds, the cruelty and abominable practice attending such courts are sufficiently apparent. There was also a circumstance in the constitution of these parliaments, but little known in England, and which, under such a government as that of France, must be considered as very singular. They had the power, and were in the constant practice of issuing decrees, without the consent of the crown, and which had the force of laws through the whole of their jurisdiction; and of all other laws, these were sure to be the best obeyed; for as all infringements of them were brought before sovereign courts, composed of the same persons who had enacted these laws (a horrible system of tyranny!) they were certain of being punished with the last severity. It must appear strange, in a government so despotic in some respects as that of France, to see the parliaments in every part of the kingdom making laws without the King's consent, and even in defiance of his authority. The English, whom I met in France in 1789, were surprized to see some of these bodies issuing arrêts against the export of corn out out of the provinces subject to their jurisdiction, into the neighbouring provinces, at the same time that the King, through the organ of so popular a minister as Mons. Necker, was decreeing an absolutely free transport of corn throughout the kingdom, and even at the requisition of the National Assembly itself. But this was nothing new; it was their common practice. The parliament of Rouen passed an arrêt against killing of calves; it was a preposterous one, and opposed by administration; but it had its full force; and had a butcher dared to offend against it, he would have found, by the rigour of his punishment, who was his master. Innoculation was favoured by the court in Louis XV.'s time; but the parliament of Paris passed an arrêt against it, much more effective in prohibiting, than the favour of the court in encouraging that practice. Instances are innumerable, and I may remark, that the bigotry, ignorance, false principles, and tyranny of these bodies were generally conspicuous; and that the court (taxation excepted), never had a dispute with a parliament, but the parliament was sure to be wrong. Their constitution, in respect to the administration of justice, was so truly rotten, that the members sat as judges, even in causes of private property, in which they were themselves the parties, and have, in this capacity, been guilty of oppressions and cruelties, which the crown has rarely dared to attempt.

It is impossible to justify the excesses of the people on their taking up arms; they were certainly guilty of cruelties; it is idle to deny the facts, for they have been proved too clearly to admit of a doubt. But is it really the people to whom we are to impute the whole?—Or to their oppressors who had kept them so long in a state of bondage? He who chooses to be served by slaves, and by ill-treated slaves, must know that he holds both his property and life by a tenure far different from those who prefer the service of well treated freemen; and he who dines to the music of groaning sufferers, must not, in the moment of insurrection, complain that his daughters are ravished, and then destroyed; and that his sons' throats are cut. When such evils happen, they surely are more imputable to the tyranny of the master, than to the cruelty of the servant. The analogy holds with the French peasants—the murder of a seigneur, or a chateau in flames, is recorded in every newspaper; the rank of the person who suffers, attracts notice; but where do we find the register of that seigneur's oppressions of his peasantry, and his exactions of feudal services, from those whose children were dying around them for want of bread?25Where do we find the minutes that assigned these starving wretches to some vile petty-fogger, to be fleeced by impositions, and a mockery of justice, in the seigneural courts? Who gives us the awards of the intendant and hissub-delegués, which took off the taxes of a man of fashion, and laid them with accumulated weight, on the poor, who were so unfortunate as to be his neighbours? Who has dwelt sufficiently upon explaining all the ramifications of despotism, regal, aristocratical, and ecclesiastical, pervading the whole mass of the people; reaching, like a circulating fluid, the most distant capillary tubes of poverty and wretchedness?

In these cases, the sufferers are too ignoble to be known; and the mass too indiscriminate to be pitied. But should a philosopher feel and reason thus? should he mistake the cause for the effect? and giving all his pity to the few, feel no compassion for the many, because they suffer in his eyes not individually, but by millions? The excesses of the people cannot, I repeat, be justified; it would undoubtedly have done them credit, both as men and christians, if they had possessed their new acquired power with moderation. But let it be remembered, that the populace in no country ever use power with moderation; excess is inherent in their aggregate constitution: and as every government in the world knows, that violence infallibly attends power in such hands, it is doubly bound in common sense, and for common safety, so to conduct itself, that the people may not find an interest in public confusions. They will always suffer much and long, before they are effectually roused; nothing, therefore, can kindle the flame, but such oppressions of some classes or order in the society, as give able men the opportunity of seconding the general mass; discontent will soon diffuse itself around; and if the government take not warning in time, it is alone answerable for all the burnings, and plunderings, and devastation, and blood that follow. The true judgment to be formed of the French revolution, must surely be gained, from an attentive consideration of the evils of the old government: when these are well understood—and when the extent and universality of the oppression under which the people groaned—oppression which bore upon them from every quarter, it will scarcely be attempted to be urged, that a revolution was not absolutely necessary to the welfare of the kingdom. Not one opposing voice26can, with reason, be raised against this assertion: abuses ought certainly to be corrected, and corrected effectually: this could not be done without the establishment of a new form of government; whether the form that has been adopted were the best, is another question absolutely distinct. But that the above-mentioned detail of enormities practised on the people required some great change is sufficiently apparent; and I cannot better conclude such a list of detestable oppressions, than in the words of the Tiers Etat of Nivernois, who hailed the approaching day of liberty, with an eloquence worthy of the subject.

Having seen the propriety, or rather the necessity, of some change in the government, let us next briefly inquire into the effects of the revolution on the principal interests in the kingdom.

In respect to all the honours, power, and profit derived to the nobility from the feudal system, which was of an extent in France beyond anything known in England since the revolution, or long parliament of 1640, all is laid in the dust, without a rag or remnant being spared:27the importance of these, both in influence and revenue, was so great, that the result is all but ruin to numbers. However, as these properties were really tyrannies; as they rendered the possession of one spot of land ruinous to all round it—and equally subversive of agriculture, and the common rights of mankind, the utter destruction brought on all this species of property, does not ill deserve the epithet they are so fond of in France; it is a real regeneration of the people to the privileges of human nature. No man of common feelings can regret the fall of all of that abominable system, which made a whole parish slaves to the lord of the manor. But the effects of the revolution have gone much farther; and have been attended with consequences not equally justifiable. The rents of land, which are as legal under the new government as they were under the old, are no longer paid with regularity. I have been lately informed (August 1791), on authority not to be doubted, that associations among tenantry, to a great amount and extent, have been formed, even within fifty miles of Paris, for the non-payment of rent;

saying, in direct terms, we are strong enough to detain the rent, and you are not strong enough to enforce the payment. In a country where such things are possible, property of every kind it must be allowed, is in a dubious situation. Very evil consequences will result from this; arrears will accumulate too great for landlords to lose, or for the peasants to pay, who will not easily be brought to relish that order and legal government, which must necessarily secure these arrears to their right owners.

The ill effects of the revolution have been felt more severely by the manufacturers of the kingdom, than by any other class of the people. The rivalry of the English fabrics in 1787 and 1788, was strong and successful; and the confusions that followed in all parts of the kingdom, had the effect of lessening the incomes of so many landlords, clergy, and men in public employments; and such numbers fled from the kingdom, that the general mass of the consumption of national fabrics sunk perhaps three- fourths. The men, whose incomes were untouched, lessened their consumption greatly, from an apprehension of the unsettled state of things: the prospects of a civil war, suggested to every man, that his safety, perhaps his future bread, depended on the money which he could hoard. The inevitable consequence, was turning absolutely out of employment immense numbers of workmen. I have, in the diary of the journey, noticed the misery to which I was a witness at Lyons, Abbeville, Amiens, &c. and by intelligence, I understood that it was still worse at Rouen: the fact could hardly be otherwise. This effect, which was absolute death, by starving many thousands of families, was a result, that, in my opinion, might have been avoided. It flowed only from carrying things to extremities—from driving the nobility out of the kingdom, and seizing, instead of regulating, the whole regal authority. These violences were not necessary to liberty; they even destroyed true liberty, by giving the government of the kingdom, in too great a degree, to Paris, and to the populace of every town.

The effect of the revolution, to the small proprietors of the kingdom, must, according to common nature of events, be, in the end, remarkably happy; and had the new government adopted any principles of taxation, except those of the economistes, establishing at the same time an absolute freedom in the business of inclosure, and in the police of corn, the result would probably have been advantageous, even at this recent period. The committee of imposts48mention (and I doubt not their accuracy), the prosperity of agriculture, in the same page in which they lament the depression of every other brance of the national industry. Upon a moderate calculation, there remained, in the hands of the classes depending on land, on the account of taxes in the years 1789 and 1790, at least 300,000,000 liv.; the execution of corvéeswas as lax as the payment of taxes. To this we are to add two years' tythe, which I cannot estimate at less than 300,000,000 liv. more. The abolition of all feudal rents, and payments of every sort during those two years, could not be less than 100,000,000 liv. including services. But all these articles, great as they were, amounting to near 800,000,000 liv. were less than the immense sums that came into the hands of the farmers by the high price of corn throughout the year 1789; a price arising almost entirely from Mons. Necker's fine operations in the corn trade, as it has been proved at large; it is true there is a deduction to be made on account of the unavoidable diminution of consumption in every article of land produce, not essentially necessary to life: every object of luxury, or tending to it, is lessened greatly. But after this discount is allowed, the balance, in favour of the little proprietor farmers, must be very great. The benefit of such a sum being added, as it is to the capital of husbandry, needs no explanation. Their agriculture must be invigorated by such wealth—by the freedom enjoyed by its its professors; by the destruction of its innumerable shackles; and even by the distresses of other employments, occasioning new and great investments of capital in land: and these leading facts will appear in a clearer light, when the prodigious division of landed property in France is well considered; probably half, perhaps two- thirds, of the kingdom are in the possession of little proprietors, who paid quit-rents, and feudal duties, for the spots they farmed. Such men are placed at once in comparative affluence; and as ease is thus acquired by at least half the kingdom, it must not be set down as a point of trifling importance. Should France escape a civil war, she will, in the prosperity of these men, find a resource which politicians at a distance do not calculate. With rents the case is certainly different; for, beyond all doubt, landlords will, sooner or later, avail themselves of these circumstances, by advancing their rents; acting in this respect, as in every other country, is common; but they will find it impossible to deprive the tenantry of a vast advantage, necessarily flowing from their emancipation.

The confusion, which has since arisen in the finances, owing almost entirely to the mode of taxation adopted by the assembly, has had the effect of continuing to the present moment (1791), a freedom from all impost to the little proprietors, which, however dreadful its general effects on the national affairs, has tended strongly to enrich this class.

The effects of the revolution, not on any particular class of cultivators, but on agriculture in general, is with me, I must confess, very questionable; I see no benefits flowing,particularlyto agriculture (liberty applies equally to allclasses, and is not yet sufficiently established for the protection of property), except the case of tythes; but I see the rise of many evils; restrictions and prohibitions on the trade of corn—a varying land-tax—and impeded inclosures, are mischiefs on principle,that may have a generative faculty; and will prove infinite drawbacks from the prosperity, which certainly was attainable. It is to be hoped, that the good sense of the assembly will reverse this system by degrees; for, if it is not reversed, AGRICULTURE CANNOT FLOURISH.

A Younger View

William Godwin (1756-1836)
Enquiry Concerning Political Justice and its
Influence on Morals and Happiness (1793)

William Blake (1757-1827)
The French Revolution (poem) (1791)

Enquiry Concerning Political Justice

William Godwin (1756-1836)

Chapter I
Systems of Political Writers

The question stated. — First hypothesis: government founded in superior strength. — Second hypothesis: government JURE DIVINO. — Third hypothesis: the social contract. — The first hypothesis examined. — The second. — Criterion of divine right: 1, patriarchal descent — 2, justice

HAVING in the preceding book attempted a general delineation of the principles of rational society, it is proper that we, in the next place, proceed to the topic of government.

It has hitherto been the persuasion of communities of men in all ages and countries that there are occasions, in which it becomes necessary, to supersede private judgement for the sake of public good, and to control the acts of the individual, by an act to be performed in the name of the whole.

Previously to our deciding upon this question, it will be of advantage to enquire into the nature of government, and the manner in which this control may be exercised with the smallest degree of violence and usurpation in regard to the individual. This point, being determined, will assist us finally to ascertain both the quantity of evil which government in its best form involves, and the urgency of the case which has been supposed to demand its interference.

There can be little ground to question the necessity, and consequently the justice, of force to be, in some cases, interposed between individual and individual. Violence is so prompt a mode of deciding differences of opinion and contentions of passion that there will infallibly be some persons who will resort to this mode. How is their violence to be repressed, or prevented from being accompanied occasionally with the most tragical effects? Violence must necessarily be preceded by an opinion of the mind dictating that violence; and, as he who first has resort to force instead of argument, is unquestionably erroneous, the best and most desirable mode of correcting him is by convincing him of his error. But the urgency of the case when, for example, a dagger is pointed to my own breast or that of another, may be such as not to afford time for expostulation. Hence the propriety and duty of defence.

Is not defence equally necessary, on the part of a community, against a foreign enemy, or the contumacy of its own members? This is perhaps the most forcible view in which the argument in favour of the institution of government has yet been placed. But, waiving this question for the present, the enquiry now proposed is, if action on the part of the community should in any in stance be found requisite, in what manner is it proper or just that the force, acting in behalf of the community, should be organized?

There are three hypotheses that have been principally maintained upon this subject. First, the system of force, according to which it is affirmed "that, inasmuch as it is necessary that the great mass of mankind should be held under the subjection of compulsory restraint, there can be no other criterion of that restraint than the power of the individuals who lay claim to its exercise, the foundation of which power exists, in the unequal degrees in which corporal strength, and intellectual sagacity, are distributed among mankind."

There is a second class of reasoners, who deduce the origin of all government from divine right, and affirm "that, as men derived their existence from an infinite creator at first, so are they still subject to his providential care, and of consequence owe allegiance to their civil governors, as to a power which he has thought fit to set over them."

The third system is that which has been most usually maintained by the friends of equality and justice; the system according to which the individuals of any society are supposed to have entered into a contract with their governors or with each other, and which founds the authority of government in the consent of the governed.

The first two of these hypotheses may easily be dismissed. That of force appears to proceed upon the total negation of abstract and immutable justice, affirming every government to be right that is possessed of power sufficient to enforce its decrees. It puts a violent termination upon all political science; and is calculated for nothing further than to persuade men to sit down quietly under their present disadvantages, whatever they may be, and not exert themselves to discover a remedy for the evils they suffer. The second hypothesis is of an equivocal nature. It either coincides with the first, and affirms all existing power to be alike of divine derivation; or it must remain totally useless, till a criterion can be found to distinguish those governments which are approved by God from those which cannot lay claim to that sanction. The criterion of patriarchal descent will be of no avail till the true claimant and rightful heir can be discovered. If we make utility and justice the test of God's approbation, this hypothesis will be liable to little objection; but then on the other hand little will be gained by it, since those who have not introduced divine right into the argument will yet readily grant that a government which can be shown to be agreeable to utility and justice is a rightful government.

The third hypothesis demands a more careful examination. If any error have insinuated itself into the support of truth, it becomes of particular consequence to detect it. Nothing can be of more importance than to separate prejudice and mistake on the one hand from reason and demonstration on the other. Wherever they have been confounded, the cause of truth must necessarily be the sufferer. The cause, so far from being injured by a dissolution of the unnatural alliance, may be expected to derive from that dissolution a superior degree of prosperity and lustre.

Chapter II
Of the Social Contract

Queries proposed. — Who are the contracting parties? — What is the form of engagement? Over how long a period does the contract extend? — To how great a variety of propositions? — Can it extend to laws hereafter to be made? — Addresses of adhesion considered. Power of a majority.

UPON the first statement of the system of a social contract various difficulties present themselves. Who are the parties to this contract? For whom did they consent, for themselves only, or for others? For how long a time is this contract to be considered as binding? If the consent of every individual be necessary, in what manner is that consent to be given? Is it to be tacit, or declared in express terms?

Little will be gained for the cause of equality and justice if our ancestors, at the first institution of government, had a right indeed of choosing the system of regulations under which they thought proper to live, but at the same time could barter away the understandings and independence of all that came after them, to the latest posterity. But, if the contract must be renewed in each successive generation, what periods must be fixed on for that purpose? And if I be obliged to submit to the established government till my turn comes to assent to it, upon what principle is that obligation founded? Surely not upon the contract into which my father entered before I was born?

Secondly, what is the nature of the consent in consequence of which I am to be reckoned a party to the frame of any political constitution? It is usually said "that acquiescence is sufficient; and that this acquiescence is to be inferred from my living quietly under the protection of the laws." But if this be true, an end is as effectually put to all political science, all discrimination of better and worse, as by any system invented by the most slavish sycophant. Upon this hypothesis every government that is quietly submitted to is a lawful government, whether it be the usurpation of Cromwell, or the tyranny of Caligula. Acquiescence is frequently nothing more, than a choice on the part of the individual, of what he deems the least evil. In many cases it is not so much as this, since the peasant and the artisan, who form the bulk of a nation, however dissatisfied with the government of their country, seldom have it in their power to transport themselves to another. It is also to be observed upon the system of acquiescence, that it is in little agreement with the established opinions and practices of mankind. Thus what has been called the law of nations, lays least stress upon the allegiance of a foreigner settling among us, though his acquiescence is certainly most complete; while natives removing into an uninhabited region are claimed by the mother country, and removing into a neighbouring territory are punished by municipal law, if they take arms against the country in which they were born. But surely acquiescence can scarcely be construed into consent, while the individuals concerned are wholly unapprised of the authority intended to be rested upon it.

Locke, the great champion of the doctrine of an original contract, has been aware of this difficulty, and therefore observes that "a tacit consent indeed obliges a man to obey the laws of any government, as long as he has any possessions, or enjoyment of any part of the dominions of that government; but nothing can make a man a member of the commonwealth, but his actually entering into it by positive engagement and express promise and compact." A singular distinction! implying upon the face of it that an acquiescence, such as has just been described is sufficient to render a man amenable to the penal regulations of society; but that his own consent is necessary to entitle him to the privileges of a citizen.

A third objection to the social contract will suggest itself, as soon as we attempt to ascertain the extent of the obligation, even supposing it to have been entered into in the most solemn manner by every member of the community. Allowing that I am called upon, at the period of my coming of age for example, to declare my assent or dissent to any system of opinions, or any code of practical institutes; for how long a period does this declaration bind me? Am I precluded from better information for the whole course of my life? And, if not for my whole life, why for a year, a week or even an hour? If my deliberate judgement, or my real sentiment, be of no avail in the case, in what sense can it be affirmed that all lawful government is founded in consent?

But the question of time is not the only difficulty. If you demand my assent to any proposition, it is necessary that the proposition should be stated simply and clearly. So numerous are the varieties of human understanding, in all cases where its independence and integrity are sufficiently preserved, that there is little chance of any two men coming to a precise agreement, about ten successive propositions that are in their own nature open to debate. What then can be more absurd, than to present to me the laws of England in fifty volumes folio, and call upon me to give an honest and uninfluenced vote upon their contents?

But the social contract, considered as the foundation of civil government, requires of me more than this. I am not only obliged to consent to all the laws that are actually upon record, but to all the laws that shall hereafter be made. It was under this view of the subject that Rousseau, in tracing the consequences of the social contract, was led to assert that "the great body of the people in whom the sovereign authority resides can neither delegate nor resign it. The essence of that authority," he adds, "is the general will; and will cannot be represented. It must either be the same or another; there is no alternative. The deputies of the people cannot be its representatives; they are merely its attorneys. The laws which the community does not ratify in person, are no laws, are nullities."

The difficulty here stated, has been endeavoured to be provided against by some late advocates for liberty, in the way of addresses of adhesion; addresses originating in the various districts and departments of a nation, and without which no regulation of constitutional importance is to be deemed valid. But this is a very superficial remedy. The addressers of course have seldom any other alternative, than that above alluded to, of indiscriminate admission or rejection. There is an infinite difference between the first deliberation, and the subsequent exercise of a negative The former is a real power, the latter is seldom more than the shadow of a power. Not to add, that addresses are a most precarious and equivocal mode of collecting the sense of a nation. They are usually voted in a tumultuous and summary manner; they are carried along by the tide of party; and the signatures annexed to them are obtained by indirect and accidental methods, while multitudes of bystanders, unless upon some extraordinary occasion, remain ignorant of or indifferent to the transaction.

Lastly, if government be founded in the consent of the people, it can have no power over any individual by whom that consent is refused. If a tacit consent be not sufficient, still less can I be deemed to have consented to a measure upon which I put an express negative. This immediately follows from the observations of Rousseau. If the people, or the individuals of whom the people is constituted, cannot delegate their authority to a representative, neither can any individual delegate his authority to a majority, in an assembly of which he is himself a member. That must surely be a singular species of consent, the external indications of which are often to be found, in an unremitting opposition in the first instance, and compulsory subjection in the second.

Chapter IV
Of Political Authority

Common deliberation the true foundation of government — proved from the equal claims of mankind — from the nature of our faculties from the object of government — from the effects of common deliberation. — Delegation vindicatcd. — Difference between the doctrine here maintained and that of a social contract. — Remark.
HAVING rejected the hypotheses that have most generally been advanced as to the rational basis of a political authority, let us enquire whether we may not arrive at the same object by a simple investigation of the obvious reason of the case, without refinement of system or fiction of process.

Government then being first supposed necessary for the welfare of mankind, the most important principle that can be imagined relative to its structure seems to be this; that, as government is a transaction in the name and for the benefit of the whole, every member of the community ought to have some share in the selection of its measures. The arguments in support of this proposition are various.

First, it has already appeared that there is no satisfactory criterion marking out any man, or set of men, to preside over the rest.

Secondly, all men are partakers of the common faculty, reason; and may be supposed to have some communication with the common instructor, truth. It would be wrong in an affair of such momentous concern that any chance for additional wisdom should be rejected; nor can we tell, in many cases, till after the experiment, how eminent any individual may be found in the business of guiding and deliberating for his fellows.

Thirdly, government is a contrivance instituted for the security of individuals; and it seems both reasonable that each man should have a share in providing for his own security; and probable that partiality and cabal will by this means be most effectually excluded.

Lastly, to give each man a voice in the public concerns comes nearest to that fundamental purpose of which we should never lose sight, the uncontrolled exercise of private judgement. Each man will thus be inspired with a consciousness of his own importance, and the slavish feelings that shrink up the soul in the presence of an imagined superior will be unknown.

Admitting then the propriety of each man having a share in directing the affairs of the whole in the first instance, it seems necessary that he should concur in electing a house of representatives, if he be the member of a large state; or, even in a small one, that he should assist in the appointment of officers and administrators[50]; which implies, first, a delegation of authority to these officers, and, secondly, a tacit consent, or rather an admission of the necessity, that the questions to be debated should abide the decision of a majority.

But to this system of delegation the same objections may be urged that were cited from Rousseau under the head of a social contract. It may be alleged that "if it be the business of every man to exercise his own judgement, he can in no instance surrender this function into the hands of another."

To this objection it may be answered, first, that the parallel is by no means complete between an individual's exercise of his judgement in a case that is truly his own, and his exercise of his judgement in an article where the province of a government is already admitted. If there be something contrary to the simplest ideas of justice in such a delegation, this is an evil inseparable from political government. The true and only adequate apology of government is necessity; the office of common deliberation is solely to supply the most eligible means of meeting that necessity.

Secondly, the delegation we are here considering is not, as the word in its most obvious sense may seem to imply, the act of one man committing to another a function which, strictly speaking, it became him to exercise for himself. Delegation, in every instance in which it can be reconciled with justice, proposes for its object the general good. The individuals to whom the delegation is made are either more likely, from talents or leisure, to perform the function in the most eligible manner, or there is at least some public interest requiring that it should be performed by one or a few persons, rather than by every individual for himself. This is the case whether in that first and simplest of all political delegations, the prerogative of a majority, or in the election of a house of representatives, or in the appointment of public officers. Now all contest as to the person who shall exercise a certain function and the propriety of resigning it is frivolous the moment it is decided how and by whom it can most advantageously be exercised. It is of no consequence that I am the parent of a child when it has once been ascertained that the child will live with greater benefit under the superintendence of a stranger.

Lastly, it is a mistake to imagine that the propriety of restraining me, when my conduct is injurious, rises out of any delegation of mine. The justice of employing force upon certain emergencies was at least equally cogent before the existence of society. Force ought never to be resorted to but in cases of absolute necessity; and, when such cases occur, it is the duty of every man to defend himself from violation. There is therefore no delegation necessary on the part of the offender; but the community, in the censure it exercises over him, puts itself in the place of the injured party.

From what is here stated, we may be enabled to form the clearest and most unexceptionable idea of the nature of government. Every man, as was formerly observed, has a sphere of discretion; that sphere is limited by the co-ordinate sphere of his neighbour. The maintenance of this limitation, the office of taking care that no man exceeds his sphere, is the first business of government. Its powers, in this respect, are a combination of the powers of individuals to control the excesses of each other. Hence is derived to the individuals of the community a second and indirect province, of providing, by themselves or their representatives, that this control is not exercised in a despotical manner, or carried to an undue excess.

It may perhaps be imagined by some persons that the doctrine here delivered, of the justice of proceeding in common concerns by a common deliberation, is nearly coincident with that which affirms a lawful government to derive its authority from a social contract. Let us consider what is the true difference between them: and this seems principally to lie in the following particular.

The principle of a social contract is an engagement to which a man is bound by honour, fidelity or consistency to adhere. According to the principle here laid down, he is bound to nothing. He joins in the common deliberation because he foresees that some authority will be exercised, and because this is the best chance that offers itself for approximating the exercise of that authority, to the dictates of his own understanding. But, when the deliberation is over, he finds himself as much disengaged as ever. If he conform to the mandate of authority, it is either because he individually approves it, or from a principle of prudence, because he foresees that a greater mass of evil will result from his disobedience than of good. He obeys the freest and best constituted authority, upon the same principle that would lead him, in most instances, to yield obedience to a despotism; only with this difference, that, if the act of authority be erroneous, he finds it less probable that it will be corrected in the first instance than in the second, since it proceeds from the erroneous judgement of a whole people. — But all this will appear with additional evidence when we come to treat of the subject of obedience.

Too much stress has undoubtedly been laid upon the idea, as of a grand and magnificent spectacle, of a nation deciding for itself upon some great public principle, and of the highest magistracy yielding its claims when the general voice has pronounced. The value of the whole must at last depend upon the quality of their decision. Truth cannot be made more true by the number of its votaries. Nor is the spectacle much less interesting of a solitary individual, bearing his undaunted testimony in favour of justice, though opposed by misguided millions. Within certain limits however the beauty of the exhibition may be acknowledged. That a nation should exercise undiminished its function of common deliberation is a step gained, and a step that inevitably leads to an improvement of the character of individuals. That men should agree in the assertion of truth is no unpleasing evidence of their virtue. Lastly, that an individual, however great may be his imaginary elevation, should be obliged to yield his personal pretensions to the sense of the community at least bears the appearance of a practical confirmation of the great principle that all private considerations must yield to the general good.

The French Revolution (poem) (1791)

William Blake (1757-1827)

A Poem,
In Seven Books.
Book the First.

Book the First
(Printed 1791)

THE DEAD brood over Europe: the cloud and vision descends over cheerful France;
O cloud well appointed! Sick, sick, the Prince on his couch! wreath'd in dim
And appalling mist; his strong hand outstretch'd, from his shoulder down the bone,
Runs aching cold into the sceptre, too heavy for mortal grasp—no more
To be swayèd by visible hand, nor in cruelty bruise the mild flourishing mountains.

Sick the mountains! and all their vineyards weep, in the eyes of the kingly mourner;
Pale is the morning cloud in his visage. Rise, Necker! the ancient dawn calls us
To awake from slumbers of five thousand years. I awake, but my soul is in dreams;
From my window I see the old mountains of France, like agèd men, fading away.

Troubled, leaning on Necker, descends the King to his chamber of council; shady mountains
In fear utter voices of thunder; the woods of France embosom the sound;
Clouds of wisdom prophetic reply, and roll over the palace roof heavy.
Forty men, each conversing with woes in the infinite shadows of his soul,
Like our ancient fathers in regions of twilight, walk, gathering round the King:

Again the loud voice of France cries to the morning; the morning prophesies to its clouds.

For the Commons convene in the Hall of the Nation. France shakes! And the heavens of France
Perplex'd vibrate round each careful countenance! Darkness of old times around them
Utters loud despair, shadowing Paris; her grey towers groan, and the Bastille trembles.
In its terrible towers the Governor stood, in dark fogs list'ning the horror;
A thousand his soldiers, old veterans of France, breathing red clouds of power and dominion.
Sudden seiz'd with howlings, despair, and black night, he stalk'd like a lion from tower
To tower; his howlings were heard in the Louvre; from court to court restless he dragg'd
His strong limbs; from court to court curs'd the fierce torment unquell'd,
Howling and giving the dark command; in his soul stood the purple plague,
Tugging his iron manacles, and piercing thro' the seven towers dark and sickly,
Panting over the prisoners like a wolf gorg'd. And the den nam'd Horror held a man
Chain'd hand and foot; round his neck an iron band, bound to the impregnable wall;
In his soul was the serpent coil'd round in his heart, hid from the light, as in a cleft rock:
And the man was confin'd for a writing prophetic. In the tower nam'd Darkness was a man
Pinion'd down to the stone floor, his strong bones scarce cover'd with sinews; the iron rings
Were forg'd smaller as the flesh decay'd: a mask of iron on his face hid the lineaments
Of ancient Kings, and the frown of the eternal lion was hid from the oppressèd earth.
In the tower namèd Bloody, a skeleton yellow remainèd in its

chains on its couch
Of stone, once a man who refus'd to sign papers of abhorrence; the eternal worm
Crept in the skeleton. In the den nam'd Religion, a loathsome sick woman bound down
To a bed of straw; the seven diseases of earth, like birds of prey, stood on the couch
And fed on the body: she refus'd to be whore to the Minister, and with a knife smote him.
In the tower nam'd Order, an old man, whose white beard cover'd the stone floor like weeds
On margin of the sea, shrivell'd up by heat of day and cold of night; his den was short
And narrow as a grave dug for a child, with spider's webs wove, and with slime
Of ancient horrors cover'd, for snakes and scorpions are his companions; harmless they breathe
His sorrowful breath: he, by conscience urg'd, in the city of Paris rais'd a pulpit,
And taught wonders to darken'd souls. In the den nam'd Destiny a strong man sat,
His feet and hands cut off, and his eyes blinded; round his middle a chain and a band
Fasten'd into the wall; fancy gave him to see an image of despair in his den,
Eternally rushing round, like a man on his hands and knees, day and night without rest:
He was friend to the favourite. In the seventh tower, nam'd the tower of God, was a man
Mad, with chains loose, which he dragg'd up and down; fed with hopes year by year, he pinèd
For liberty.—Vain hopes! his reason decay'd, and the world of attraction in his bosom
Centred, and the rushing of chaos overwhelm'd his dark soul: he was confin'd
For a letter of advice to a King, and his ravings in winds are heard over Versailles.

But the dens shook and trembled: the prisoners look up and
assay to shout; they listen,
Then laugh in the dismal den, then are silent; and a light
walks round the dark towers.
For the Commons convene in the Hall of the Nation; like
spirits of fire in the beautiful
Porches of the Sun, to plant beauty in the desert craving
abyss, they gleam
On the anxious city: all children new-born first behold them,
tears are fled,
And they nestle in earth-breathing bosoms. So the city of
Paris, their wives and children,
Look up to the morning Senate, and visions of sorrow leave
pensive streets.

But heavy-brow'd jealousies lour o'er the Louvre; and terrors
of ancient Kings
Descend from the gloom and wander thro' the palace, and
weep round the King and his Nobles;
While loud thunders roll, troubling the dead. Kings are sick
throughout all the earth!
The voice ceas'd: the Nation sat; but ancient darkness and
trembling wander thro' the palace.

As in day of havoc and routed battle, among thick shades of
discontent,
On the soul-skirting mountains of sorrow cold waving, the
Nobles fold round the King;
Each stern visage lock'd up as with strong bands of iron, each
strong limb bound down as with marble,
In flames of red wrath burning, bound in astonishment a
quarter of an hour.

Then the King glow'd: his Nobles fold round, like the sun of
old time quench'd in clouds;
In their darkness the King stood; his heart flam'd, and utter'd a
with'ring heat, and these words burst forth:

'The nerves of five thousand years' ancestry tremble, shaking the heavens of France;
Throbs of anguish beat on brazen war foreheads; they descend and look into their graves.
I see thro' darkness, thro' clouds rolling round me, the spirits of ancient Kings
Shivering over their bleachèd bones; round them their counsellors look up from the dust,
Crying: "Hide from the living! Our bonds and our prisoners shout in the open field.
Hide in the nether earth! Hide in the bones! Sit obscurèd in the hollow scull!
Our flesh is corrupted, and we wear away. We are not numberèd among the living. Let us hide
In stones, among roots of trees. The prisoners have burst their dens.
Let us hide! let us hide in the dust! and plague and wrath and tempest shall cease."

He ceas'd, silent pond'ring; his brows folded heavy, his forehead was in affliction.
Like the central fire from the window he saw his vast armies spread over the hills,
Breathing red fires from man to man, and from horse to horse: then his bosom
Expanded like starry heaven; he sat down: his Nobles took their ancient seats.

Then the ancientest Peer, Duke of Burgundy, rose from the Monarch's right hand, red as wines
From his mountains; an odour of war, like a ripe vineyard, rose from his garments,
And the chamber became as a clouded sky; o'er the Council he stretch'd his red limbs
Cloth'd in flames of crimson; as a ripe vineyard stretches over sheaves of corn,
The fierce Duke hung over the Council; around him crowd, weeping in his burning robe,

A bright cloud of infant souls: his words fall like purple autumn on the sheaves:

'Shall this marble-built heaven become a clay cottage, this earth an oak stool, and these mowers
From the Atlantic mountains mow down all this great starry harvest of six thousand years?
And shall Necker, the hind of Geneva, stretch out his crook'd sickle o'er fertile France,
Till our purple and crimson is faded to russet, and the kingdoms of earth bound in sheaves,
And the ancient forests of chivalry hewn, and the joys of the combat burnt for fuel;
Till the power and dominion is rent from the pole, sword and sceptre from sun and moon,
The law and gospel from fire and air, and eternal reason and science
From the deep and the solid, and man lay his faded head down on the rock
Of eternity, where the eternal lion and eagle remain to devour?
This to prevent, urg'd by cries in day, and prophetic dreams hovering in night,
To enrich the lean earth that craves, furrow'd with ploughs, whose seed is departing from her,
Thy Nobles have gather'd thy starry hosts round this rebellious city,
To rouse up the ancient forests of Europe, with clarions of cloud-breathing war,
To hear the horse neigh to the drum and trumpet, and the trumpet and war shout reply.
Stretch the hand that beckons the eagles of heaven: they cry over Paris, and wait
Till Fayette point his finger to Versailles—the eagles of heaven must have their prey!'

He ceas'd, and burn'd silent: red clouds roll round Necker; a weeping is heard o'er the palace.

Like a dark cloud Necker paus'd, and like thunder on the just man's burial day he paus'd.
Silent sit the winds, silent the meadows; while the husbandman and woman of weakness
And bright children look after him into the grave, and water his clay with love,
Then turn towards pensive fields: so Necker paus'd, and his visage was cover'd with clouds.

The King lean'd on his mountains; then lifted his head and look'd on his armies, that shone
Thro' heaven, tinging morning with beams of blood; then turning to Burgundy, troubled:—
'Burgundy, thou wast born a lion! My soul is o'ergrown with distress
For the Nobles of France, and dark mists roll round me and blot the writing of God
Written in my bosom. Necker rise! leave the kingdom, thy life is surrounded with snares.
We have call'd an Assembly, but not to destroy; we have given gifts, not to the weak;
I hear rushing of muskets and bright'ning of swords; and visages, redd'ning with war,
Frowning and looking up from brooding villages and every dark'ning city.
Ancient wonders frown over the kingdom, and cries of women and babes are heard,
And tempests of doubt roll around me, and fierce sorrows, because of the Nobles of France.
Depart! answer not! for the tempest must fall, as in years that are passèd away.'

Dropping a tear the old man his place left, and when he was gone out
He set his face toward Geneva to flee; and the women and children of the city
Kneel'd round him and kissèd his garments and wept: he stood a short space in the street,

Then fled; and the whole city knew he was fled to Geneva, and the Senate heard it.

But the Nobles burn'd wrathful at Necker's departure, and wreath'd their clouds and waters
In dismal volumes; as, risen from beneath, the Archbishop of Paris arose
In the rushing of scales, and hissing of flames, and rolling of sulphurous smoke:—

'Hearken, Monarch of France, to the terrors of heaven, and let thy soul drink of my counsel!
Sleeping at midnight in my golden tower, the repose of the labours of men
Wav'd its solemn cloud over my head. I awoke; a cold hand passèd over my limbs, and behold!
An agèd form, white as snow, hov'ring in mist, weeping in the uncertain light.
Dim the form almost faded, tears fell down the shady cheeks; at his feet many cloth'd
In white robes, strewn in air censers and harps, silent they lay prostrated;
Beneath, in the awful void, myriads descending and weeping thro' dismal winds;
Endless the shady train shiv'ring descended, from the gloom where the agèd form wept.
At length, trembling, the vision sighing, in a low voice like the voice of the grasshopper, whisper'd:
"My groaning is heard in the abbeys, and God, so long worshipp'd, departs as a lamp
Without oil; for a curse is heard hoarse thro' the land, from a godless race
Descending to beasts; they look downward, and labour, and forget my holy law;
The sound of prayer fails from lips of flesh, and the holy hymn from thicken'd tongues;
For the bars of Chaos are burst; her millions prepare their fiery way

Thro' the orbèd abode of the holy dead, to root up and pull
down and remove,
And Nobles and Clergy shall fail from before me, and my
cloud and vision be no more;
The mitre become black, the crown vanish, and the sceptre
and ivory staff
Of the ruler wither among bones of death; they shall consume
from the thistly field,
And the sound of the bell, and voice of the sabbath, and
singing of the holy choir
Is turn'd into songs of the harlot in day, and cries of the virgin
in night.
They shall drop at the plough and faint at the harrow,
unredeem'd, unconfess'd, unpardon'd;
The priest rot in his surplice by the lawless lover, the holy
beside the accursèd,
The King, frowning in purple, beside the grey ploughman, and
their worms embrace together."
The voice ceas'd: a groan shook my chamber. I slept, for the
cloud of repose returnèd;
But morning dawn'd heavy upon me. I rose to bring my Prince
heaven-utter'd counsel.
Hear my counsel, O King! and send forth thy Generals; the
command of Heaven is upon thee!
Then do thou command, O King! to shut up this Assembly in
their final home;
Let thy soldiers possess this city of rebels, that threaten to
bathe their feet
In the blood of Nobility, trampling the heart and the head; let
the Bastille devour
These rebellious seditious; seal them up, O Anointed! in
everlasting chains.'
He sat down: a damp cold pervaded the Nobles, and
monsters of worlds unknown
Swam round them, watching to be deliverèd—when Aumont,
whose chaos-born soul
Eternally wand'ring, a comet and swift-falling fire, pale enter'd
the chamber.

Before the red Council he stood, like a man that returns from hollow graves:—

'Awe-surrounded, alone thro' the army, a fear and a with'ring blight blown by the north,
The Abbé de Sieyes from the Nation's Assembly, O Princes and Generals of France,
Unquestionèd, unhinderèd! Awe-struck are the soldiers; a dark shadowy man in the form
Of King Henry the Fourth walks before him in fires; the captains like men bound in chains
Stood still as he pass'd: he is come to the Louver, O King, with a message to thee!
The strong soldiers tremble, the horses their manes bow, and the guards of thy palace are fled!'

Uprose awful in his majestic beams Bourbon's strong Duke; his proud sword, from his thigh
Drawn, he threw on the earth: the Duke of Bretagne and the Earl of Bourgogne
Rose inflam'd, to and fro in the chamber, like thunder-clouds ready to burst.

'What damp all our fires, O spectre of Henry!' said Bourbon, 'and rend the flames
From the head of our King? Rise, Monarch of France! command me, and I will lead
This army of superstition at large, that the ardour of noble souls, quenchless,
May yet burn in France, nor our shoulders be plough'd with the furrows of poverty.'

Then Orleans, generous as mountains, arose and unfolded his robe, and put forth
His benevolent hand, looking on the Archbishop, who changèd as pale as lead,
Would have risen but could not: his voice issuèd harsh grating; instead of words harsh hissings

Shook the chamber; he ceas'd abash'd. Then Orleans spoke;
all was silent.
He breath'd on them, and said: 'O Princes of fire, whose
flames are for growth, not consuming,
Fear not dreams, fear not visions, nor be you dismay'd with
sorrows which flee at the morning!
Can the fires of Nobility ever be quench'd, or the stars by a
stormy night?
Is the body diseas'd when the members are healthful? can the
man be bound in sorrow
Whose ev'ry function is fill'd with its fiery desire? can the soul,
whose brain and heart
Cast their rivers in equal tides thro' the great Paradise,
languish because the feet,
Hands, head, bosom, and parts of love follow their high
breathing joy?
And can Nobles be bound when the people are free, or God
weep when his children are happy?
Have you never seen Fayette's forehead, or Mirabeau's eyes,
or the shoulders of Target,
Or Bailly the strong foot of France, or Clermont the terrible
voice, and your robes
Still retain their own crimson?—Mine never yet faded, for fire
delights in its form!
But go, merciless man, enter into the infinite labyrinth of
another's brain
Ere thou measure the circle that he shall run. Go, thou cold
recluse, into the fires
Of another's high flaming rich bosom, and return unconsum'd,
and write laws.
If thou canst not do this, doubt thy theories, learn to consider
all men as thy equals,
Thy brethren, and not as thy foot or thy hand, unless thou first
fearest to hurt them.'

The Monarch stood up; the strong Duke his sword to its
golden scabbard return'd;
The Nobles sat round like clouds on the mountains, when the

storm is passing away:—
'Let the Nation's Ambassador come among Nobles, like
incense of the valley!'

Aumont went out and stood in the hollow porch, his ivory
wand in his hand;
A cold orb of disdain revolv'd round him, and coverèd his soul
with snows eternal.
Great Henry's soul shudderèd, a whirlwind and fire tore
furious from his angry bosom;
He indignant departed on horses of heav'n. Then the Abbé de
Sieyes rais'd his feet
On the steps of the Louvre; like a voice of God following a
storm, the Abbé follow'd
The pale fires of Aumont into the chamber; as a father that
bows to his son,
Whose rich fields inheriting spread their old glory, so the voice
of the people bowèd
Before the ancient seat of the kingdom and mountains to be
renewèd.

'Hear, O heavens of France! the voice of the people, arising
from valley and hill,
O'erclouded with power. Hear the voice of valleys, the voice of
meek cities,
Mourning oppressèd on village and field, till the village and
field is a waste.
For the husbandman weeps at blights of the fife, and blasting
of trumpets consume
The souls of mild France; the pale mother nourishes her child
to the deadly slaughter.
When the heavens were seal'd with a stone, and the terrible
sun clos'd in an orb, and the moon
Rent from the nations, and each star appointed for watchers
of night,
The millions of spirits immortal were bound in the ruins of
sulphur heaven
To wander enslav'd; black, despress'd in dark ignorance, kept

in awe with the whip
To worship terrors, bred from the blood of revenge and breath
of desire
In bestial forms, or more terrible men; till the dawn of our
peaceful morning,
Till dawn, till morning, till the breaking of clouds, and swelling
of winds, and the universal voice;
Till man raise his darken'd limbs out of the caves of night. His
eyes and his heart
Expand—Where is Space? where; O Sun, is thy dwelling?
where thy tent, O faint slumb'rous Moon?
Then the valleys of France shall cry to the soldier: "Throw
down thy sword and musket,
And run and embrace the meek peasant." Her Nobles shall
hear and shall weep, and put off
The red robe of terror, the crown of oppression, the shoes of
contempt, and unbuckle
The girdle of war from the desolate earth. Then the Priest in
his thund'rous cloud
Shall weep, bending to earth, embracing the valleys, and
putting his hand to the plough,
Shall say: "No more I curse thee; but now I will bless thee: no
more in deadly black
Devour thy labour; nor lift up a cloud in thy heavens, O
laborious plough;
That the wild raging millions, that wander in forests, and howl
in law-blasted wastes,
Strength madden'd with slavery, honesty bound in the dens of
superstition,
May sing in the village, and shout in the harvest, and woo in
pleasant gardens
Their once savage loves, now beaming with knowledge, with
gentle awe adornèd;
And the saw, and the hammer, the chisel, the pencil, the pen,
and the instruments
Of heavenly song sound in the wilds once forbidden, to teach
the laborious ploughman
And shepherd, deliver'd from clouds of war, from pestilence,

from night-fear, from murder,
From falling, from stifling, from hunger, from cold, from slander, discontent and sloth,
That walk in beasts and birds of night, driven back by the sandy desert,
Like pestilent fogs round cities of men; and the happy earth sing in its course,
The mild peaceable nations be openèd to heav'n, and men walk with their fathers in bliss."
Then hear the first voice of the morning: "Depart, O clouds of night, and no more
Return; be withdrawn cloudy war, troops of warriors depart, nor around our peaceable city
Breathe fires; but ten miles from Paris let all be peace, nor a soldier be seen!"'

He ended: the wind of contention arose, and the clouds cast their shadows; the Princes
Like the mountains of France, whose agèd trees utter an awful voice, and their branches
Are shatter'd; till gradual a murmur is heard descending into the valley,
Like a voice in the vineyards of Burgundy when grapes are shaken on grass,
Like the low voice of the labouring man, instead of the shout of joy;
And the palace appear'd like a cloud driven abroad; blood ran down the ancient pillars.
Thro' the cloud a deep thunder, the Duke of Burgundy, delivers the King's command:—

'Seest thou yonder dark castle, that moated around, keeps this city of Paris in awe?
Go, command yonder tower, saying: "Bastille, depart! and take thy shadowy course;
Overstep the dark river, thou terrible tower, and get thee up into the country ten miles.
And thou black southern prison, move along the dusky road to

Versailles; there
Frown on the gardens"—and, if it obey and depart, then the
King will disband
This war-breathing army; but, if it refuse, let the Nation's
Assembly thence learn
That this army of terrors, that prison of horrors, are the bands
of the murmuring kingdom.'

Like the morning star arising above the black waves, when a
shipwreck'd soul sighs for morning,
Thro' the ranks, silent, walk'd the Ambassador back to the
Nation's Assembly, and told
The unwelcome message. Silent they heard; then a thunder
roll'd round loud and louder;
Like pillars of ancient halls and ruins of times remote, they sat.
Like a voice from the dim pillars Mirabeau rose; the thunders
subsided away;
A rushing of wings around him was heard as he brighten'd,
and cried out aloud:
'Where is the General of the Nation?' The walls re-echo'd:
  'Where is the General of the Nation?'

Sudden as the bullet wrapp'd in his fire, when brazen cannons
rage in the field,
Fayette sprung from his seat saying 'Ready!' Then bowing like
clouds, man toward man, the Assembly
Like a Council of Ardours seated in clouds, bending over the
cities of men,
And over the armies of strife, where their children are
marshall'd together to battle,
They murmuring divide; while the wind sleeps beneath, and
the numbers are counted in silence,
While they vote the removal of War, and the pestilence
weighs his red wings in the sky.

So Fayette stood silent among the Assembly, and the votes
were given, and the numbers numb'red;
And the vote was that Fayette should order the army to

remove ten miles from Paris.

The agèd Sun rises appall'd from dark mountains, and gleams
a dusky beam
On Fayette; but on the whole army a shadow, for a cloud on
the eastern hills
Hover'd, and stretch'd across the city, and across the army,
and across the Louvre.
Like a flame of fire he stood before dark ranks, and before
expecting captains:
On pestilent vapours around him flow frequent spectres of
religious men, weeping
In winds; driven out of the abbeys, their naked souls shiver in
keen open air;
Driven out by the fiery cloud of Voltaire, and thund'rous rocks
of Rousseau,
They dash like foam against the ridges of the army, uttering a
faint feeble cry.

Gleams of fire streak the heavens, and of sulphur the earth,
from Fayette as he lifted his hand;
But silent he stood, till all the officers rush round him like
waves
Round the shore of France, in day of the British flag, when
heavy cannons
Affright the coasts, and the peasant looks over the sea and
wipes a tear:
Over his head the soul of Voltaire shone fiery; and over the
army Rousseau his white cloud
Unfolded, on souls of war, living terrors, silent list'ning toward
Fayette.
His voice loud inspir'd by liberty, and by spirits of the dead,
thus thunder'd:—

'The Nation's Assembly command that the Army remove ten
miles from Paris;
Nor a soldier be seen in road or in field, till the Nation
command return.'

Rushing along iron ranks glittering, the officers each to his
station
Depart, and the stern captain strokes his proud steed, and in
front of his solid ranks
Waits the sound of trumpet; captains of foot stand each by his
cloudy drum:
Then the drum beats, and the steely ranks move, and
trumpets rejoice in the sky.
Dark cavalry, like clouds fraught with thunder, ascend on the
hills, and bright infantry, rank
Behind rank, to the soul-shaking drum and shrill fife, along the
roads glitter like fire.

The noise of trampling, the wind of trumpets, smote the
Palace walls with a blast.
Pale and cold sat the King in midst of his Peers, and his noble
heart sunk, and his pulses
Suspended their motion; a darkness crept over his eyelids,
and chill cold sweat
Sat round his brows faded in faint death; his Peers pale like
mountains of the dead,
Cover'd with dews of night, groaning, shaking forests and
floods. The cold newt,
And snake, and damp toad on the kingly foot crawl, or croak
on the awful knee,
Shedding their slime; in folds of the robe the crown'd adder
builds and hisses
From stony brows: shaken the forests of France, sick the
kings of the nations,
And the bottoms of the world were open'd, and the graves of
archangels unseal'd:
The enormous dead lift up their pale fires and look over the
rocky cliffs.

A faint heat from their fires reviv'd the cold Louvre; the frozen
blood reflow'd.
Awful uprose the King; him the Peers follow'd; they saw the

courts of the Palace
Forsaken, and Paris without a soldier, silent. For the noise was gone up
And follow'd the army; and the Senate in peace sat beneath morning's beam.

END OF THE FIRST BOOK.

A Woman's Slant

Mary Wollstonecraft (1759-1797)

A Vindication of the Rights of Men(1790)

Helen Maria Williams (1762-1827)

Letters Written in France (1790)

A Vindication of the

Rights of Men(1790)

Mary Wollstonecraft (1759-1797)

A LETTER To The Right Honourable EDMUND BURKE.

Sir,

It is not necessary, with courtly insincerity, to apologise to you for thus intruding on your precious time, not to profess that I think it an honour to discuss an important subject with a man whose literary abilities have raised him to notice in the state. I have not yet learned to twist my periods, nor, in the equivocal idiom of politeness, to disguise my sentiments, and imply what I should be afraid to utter: if, therefore, in the course of this epistle, I chance to express contempt, and even indignation, with some emphasis, I beseech you to believe that it is not a flight of fancy; for truth, in morals, has ever appeared to me the essence of the sublime; and, in taste, simplicity the only criterion of the beautiful. But I war not with an individual when I contend for the rights of menand the liberty of reason. You see I do not condescend to cull my words to avoid the invidious phrase, nor shall I be prevented from giving a manly definition of it, by the flimsy ridicule which a lively fancy has interwoven with the present acceptation of the term. Reverencing the rights of humanity, I shall dare to assert them; not intimidated by the horse laugh that you have raised, or waiting till time has wiped away the compassionate tears which you have elaborately laboured to excite.

From the many just sentiments interspersed through the letter before me, and from the whole tendency of it, I should believe you to be a good, though a vain man, if some circumstances in your conduct did not render the inflexibility of your integrity doubtful; and for this vanity a knowledge of human nature enables me to discover such extenuating circumstances, in the very texture of your mind, that I am ready to call it amiable, and separate the public from the private character.

I know that a lively imagination renders a man particularly calculated to shine in conversation and in those desultory productions where method is disregarded; and the instantaneous applause which his eloquence extorts is at once a reward and a spur. Once a wit and always a wit, is an aphorism that has received the sanction of experience; yet I am apt to conclude that the man who with scrupulous anxiety endeavours to support that shining character, can never nourish by reflection any profound, or, if you please, metaphysical passion. Ambition becomes only the tool of vanity, and his reason, the weather-cock of unrestrained feelings, is only employed to varnish over the faults which it ought to have corrected.

Sacred, however, would the infirmities and errors of a good man be, in my eyes, if they were only displayed in a private circle; if the venial fault only rendered the wit anxious, like a celebrated beauty, to raise admiration on every occasion, and excite emotion, instead of the calm reciprocation of mutual esteem and unimpassioned respect. Such vanity enlivens social intercourse, and forces the little great man to be always on his guard to secure his throne; and an ingenious man, who is ever on the watch for conquest, will, in his eagerness to exhibit his whole store of knowledge, furnish an attentive observer with some useful information, calcined by fancy and formed by taste.

And though some dry reasoner might whisper that the arguments were superficial, and should even add, that the feelings which are thus ostentatiously displayed are often the cold declamation of the head, and not the effusions of the heart–what will these shrewd remarks avail, when the witty arguments and ornamental feelings are on a level with the comprehension of the fashionable world, and a book is found very amusing? Even the Ladies, Sir, may repeat your sprightly sallies, and retail in theatrical attitudes many of your sentimental exclamations. Sensibility is the manie of the day, and compassion the virtue which is to cover a multitude of vices, whilst justice is left to mourn in sullen silence, and balance truth in vain.

In life, an honest man with a confined understanding is frequently the slave of his habits and the dupe of his feelings, whilst the man with a clearer head and colder heart makes the passions of others bend to his interest; but truly sublime is the character that acts from principle, and governs the inferior springs of activity without slackening their vigour; whose feelings give vital heat to his resolves, but never hurry him into feverish eccentricities.

However, as you have informed us that respect chills love, it is natural to conclude, that all your pretty flights arise from your pampered sensibility; and that, vain of this fancied preeminence of organs, you foster every emotion till the fumes, mounting to your brain, dispel the sober suggestions of reason. It is not in this view surprising, that when you should argue you become impassioned, and that reflection inflames your imagination, instead of enlightening your understanding.

Quitting now the flowers of rhetoric, let us, Sir, reason together; and, believe me, I should not have meddled with these troubled waters, in order to point out your inconsistencies, if your wit had not burnished up some rusty, baneful opinions, and swelled the shallow current of ridicule till it resembled the flow of reason, and presumed to be the test of truth.

I shall not attempt to follow you through 'horse-way and foot-path;' but, attacking the foundation of your opinions, I shall leave the superstructure to find a centre of gravity on which it may lean till some strong blast puffs it into the air; or your teeming fancy, which the ripening judgment of sixty years has not tamed, produces another Chinese erection, to stare, at every turn, the plain country people in the face, who bluntly call such an airy edifice—a folly.

The birthright of man, to give you, Sir, a short definition of this disputed right, is such a degree of liberty, civil and religious, as is compatible with the liberty of every other individual with whom he is united in a social compact, and the continued existence of that compact.

Liberty, in this simple, unsophisticated sense, I acknowledge, is a fair idea that has never yet received a form in the various governments that have been established on our beauteous globe; the demon of property has ever been at hand to encroach on the sacred rights of men, and to fence round with awful pomp laws that war with justice. But that it results from the eternal foundation of right–from immutable truth–who will presume to deny, that pretends to rationality–if reason has led them to build their moralityaand religion on an everlasting foundation–the attributes of God?

I glow with indignation when I attempt, methodically, to unravel your slavish paradoxes, in which I can find no fixed first principle to refute; I shall not, therefore, condescend to shew where you affirm in one page what you deny in another; and how frequently you draw conclusions without any previous premises:–it would be something like cowardice to fight with a man who had never exercised the weapons with which his opponent chose to combat, and irksome to refute sentence after sentence in which the latent spirit of tyranny appeared.

I perceive, from the whole tenor of your Reflections, that you have a mortal antipathy to reason; but, if there is anything like argument, or first principles, in your wild declamation, behold the result:–that we are to reverence the rust of antiquity, and term the unnatural customs, which ignorance and mistaken self-interest have consolidated, the sage fruit of experience: nay, that, if we do discover some errors, our feelings should lead us to excuse, with blind love, or unprincipled filial affection, the venerable vestiges of ancient days. These are gothic notions of beauty–the ivy is beautiful, but, when it insidiously destroys the trunk from which it receives support, who would not grub it up?

Further, that we ought cautiously to remain forever in frozen inactivity, because a thaw, whilst it nourishes the soil, spreads a temporary inundation; and the fear of risking any personal present convenience should prevent a struggle for the most estimable advantages. This is sound reasoning, I grant, in the mouth of the rich and short-sighted.

Yes, Sir, the strong gained riches, the few have sacrificed the many to their vices; and, to be able to pamper their appetites, and supinely exist without exercising mind or body, they have ceased to be men.–Lost to the relish of true pleasure, such beings would, indeed, deserve compassion, if injustice was not softened by the tyrant's plea–necessity; if prescription was not raised as an immortal boundary against innovation. Their minds, in fact, instead of being cultivated, have been so warped by education, that it may require some ages to bring them back to nature, and enable them to see their true interest, with that degree of conviction which is necessary to influence their conduct.

The civilization which has taken place in Europe has been very partial, and, like every custom that an arbitrary point of honour has established, refines the manners at the expence of morals, by making sentiments and opinions current in conversation that have no root in the heart, or weight in the cooler resolves of the mind.–And what has stopped its progress?– hereditary property–hereditary honours. The man has been changed into an artificial monster by the station in which he was born, and the consequent homage that benumbed his faculties like the torpedo's touch;–or a being, with a capacity of reasoning, would not have failed to discover, as his faculties unfolded, that true happiness arose from the friendship and intimacy which can only be enjoyed by equals; and that charity is not a condescending distribution of alms, but an intercourse of good offices and mutual benefits, founded on respect for justice and humanity.

Governed by these principles, the poor wretch, whose inelegant distress extorted from a mixed feeling of disgust and animal sympathy present relief, would have been considered as a man, whose misery demanded a part of his birthright, supposing him to be industrious; but should his vices have reduced him to poverty, he could only have addressed his fellow-men as weak beings, subject to like passions, who ought to forgive, because they expect to be forgiven, for suffering the impulse of the moment to silence the suggestions of conscience, or reason, which you will; for, in my view of things, they are synonymous terms.

Will Mr Burke be at the trouble to inform us, how far we are to go back to discover the rights of men, since the light of reason is such a fallacious guide that none but fools trust to its cold investigation?

In the infancy of society, confining our view to our own country, customs were established by the lawless power of an ambitious individual; or a weak prince was obliged to comply with every demand of the licentious barbarous insurgents, who disputed his authority with irrefragable arguments at the point of their swords; or the more specious requests of the Parliament, who only allowed him conditional supplies.

Are these the venerable pillars of our constitution? And is Magna Charta to rest for its chief support on a former grant, which reverts to another, till chaos becomes the base of the mighty structure—or we cannot tell what?—for coherence, without some pervading principle of order, is a solecism.

Speaking of Edward the IIId. Hume observes, that 'he was a prince of great capacity, not governed by favourites, not led astray by any unruly passion, sensible that nothing could be more essential to his interests than to keep on good terms with his people: yet, on the whole, it appears that the government, at best, was only a barbarous monarchy, not regulated by any fixed maxims, or bounded by any certain or undisputed rights, which in practice were regularly observed. The King conducted himself by one set of principles; the Barons by another; the Commons by a third; the Clergy by a fourth. All these systems of government were opposite and incompatible: each of them prevailed in its turn, as incidents were favourable to it: a great prince rendered the monarchical power predominant: the weakness of a king gave reins to the aristocracy: a superstitious age saw the clergy triumphant: the people, for whom chiefly government was instituted, and who chiefly deserve consideration, were the weakest of the whole.'

And just before that most auspicious aera, the fourteenth century, during the reign of Richard II. whose total incapacity to manage the reins of power, and keep in subjection his haughty Barons, rendered him a mere cypher; the House of Commons, to whom he was obliged frequently to apply, not only for subsidies but assistance to quell the insurrections that the contempt in which he was held naturally produced, gradually rose into power; for whenever they granted supplies to the King, they demanded in return, though it bore the name of petition, a confirmation, or the renewal of former charters, which had been infringed, and even utterly disregarded by the King and his seditious Barons, who principally held their independence of the crown by force of arms, and the encouragement which they gave to robbers and villains, who infested the country, and lived by rapine and violence.

To what dreadful extremities were the poorer sort reduced, their property, the fruit of their industry, being entirely at the disposal of their lords, who were so many petty tyrants!

In return for the supplies and assistance which the king received from the commons, they demanded privileges, which Edward, in his distress for money to prosecute the numerous wars in which he was engaged during the greater part of his reign, was constrained to grant them; so that by degrees they rose to power, and became a check on both king and nobles. Thus was the foundation of our liberty established, chiefly through the pressing necessities of the king, who was more intent on being supplied for the moment, in order to carry on his wars and ambitious projects, than aware of the blow he gave to kingly power, by thus making a body of men feel their importance, who afterwards might strenuously oppose tyranny and oppression, and effectually guard the subject's property from seizure and confiscation. Richard's weakness completed what Edward's ambition began.

At this period, it is true, Wickliffe opened a vista for reason by attacking some of the most pernicious tenets of the church of Rome; still the prospect was sufficiently misty to authorize the question—Where was the dignity of thinking of the fourteenth century?

A Roman Catholic, it is true, enlightened by the reformation, might, with singular propriety, celebrate the epoch that preceded it, to turn our thoughts from former atrocious enormities; but a Protestant must acknowledge that this faint dawn of liberty only made the subsiding darkness more visible; and that the boasted virtues of that century all bear the stamp of stupid pride and headstrong barbarism. Civility was then called condescension, and ostentatious almsgiving humanity; and men were content to borrow their virtues, or, to speak with more propriety, their consequence, from posterity, rather than undertake the arduous task of acquiring it for themselves.

The imperfection of all modern governments must, without waiting to repeat the trite remark, that all human institutions are unavoidably imperfect, in a great measure have arisen from this simple circumstance, that the constitution, if such an heterogeneous mass deserve that name, was settled in the dark days of ignorance, when the minds of men were shackled by the grossest prejudices and most immoral superstition. And do you, Sir, a sagacious philosopher, recommend night as the fittest time to analyze a ray of light?

Are we to seek for the rights of men in the ages when a few marks were the only penalty imposed for the life of a man, and death for death when the property of the rich was touched? when—I blush to discover the depravity of our nature—when a deer was killed! Are these the laws that it is natural to love, and sacrilegious to invade?—Were the rights of men understood when the law authorized or tolerated murder?—or is power and right the same in your creed?

But in fact all your declamation leads so directly to this conclusion, that I beseech you to ask your own heart, when you call yourself a friend of liberty, whether it would not be more consistent to style yourself the champion of property, the adorer of the golden image which power has set up?—And, when you are examining your heart, if it would not be too much like mathematical drudgery, to which a fine imagination very reluctantly stoops, enquire further, how it is consistent with the vulgar notions of honesty, and the foundation of morality—truth; for a man to boast of his virtue and independence, when he cannot forget that he is at the moment enjoying the wages of falsehood; band that, in a skulking, unmanly way, he has secured himself a pension of fifteen hundred pounds per annum on the Irish establishment? Do honest men, Sir, for I am not rising to the refined principle of honour, ever receive the reward of their public services, or secret assistance, in the name of another?

But to return from a digression which you will more perfectly understand than any of my readers—on what principle you, Sir, can justify the reformation, which tore up by the roots an old establishment, I cannot guess–but, I beg your pardon, perhaps you do not wish to justify it–and have some mental reservation to excuse you, to yourself, for not openly avowing your reverence. Or, to go further back;–had you been a Jew– you would have joined in the cry, crucify him!–crucify him! The promulgator of a new doctrine, and the violator of old laws and customs, that not melting, like ours, into darkness and ignorance, rested on Divine authority, must have been a dangerous innovator, in your eyes, particularly if you had not been informed that the Carpenter's Son was of the stock and lineage of David. But there is no end to the arguments which might be deduced to combat such palpable absurdities, by shewing the manifest inconsistencies which are necessarily involved in a direful train of false opinions.

It is necessary emphatically to repeat, that there are rights which men inherit at their birth, as rational creatures, who were raised above the brute creation by their improvable faculties; and that, in receiving these, not from their forefathers but, from God, prescription can never undermine natural rights.

A father may dissipate his property without his child having any right to complain;–but should he attempt to sell him for a slave, or fetter him with laws contrary to reason; nature, in enabling him to discern good from evil, teaches him to break the ignoble chain, and not to believe that bread becomes flesh, and wine blood, because his parents swallowed the Eucharist with this blind persuasion.

There is no end to this implicit submission to authority–some where it must stop, or we return to barbarism; and the capacity of improvement, which gives us a natural sceptre on earth, is a cheat, an ignis-fatuus, that leads us from inviting meadows into bogs and dung-hills. And if it be allowed that many of the precautions, with which any alteration was made, in our government, were prudent, it rather proves its weakness than substantiates an opinion of the soundness of the stamina, or the excellence of the constitution.

But on what principle Mr Burke could defend American independence, I cannot conceive; for the whole tenor of his plausible arguments settles slavery on an everlasting foundation. Allowing his servile reverence for antiquity, and prudent attention to self-interest, to have the force which he insists on, the slave trade ought never to be abolished; and, because our ignorant forefathers, not understanding the native dignity of man, sanctioned a traffic that outrages every suggestion of reason and religion, we are to submit to the inhuman custom, and term an atrocious insult to humanity the love of our country, and a proper submission to the laws by which our property is secured.–Security of property! Behold, in a few words, the definition of English liberty. And to this selfish principle every nobler one is sacrificed.–The Briton takes place of the man, and the image of God is lost in the citizen! But it is not that enthusiastic flame which in Greece and Rome consumed every sordid passion: no, self is the focus; and the disparting rays rise not above our foggy atmosphere. But softly–it is only the property of the rich that is secure; the man who lives by the sweat of his brow has no asylum from oppression; the strong man may enter–when was the castle of the poor sacred? and the base informer steal him from the family that depend on his industry for subsistence.

Fully sensible as you must be of the baneful consequences that inevitably follow this notorious infringement on the dearest rights of men, and that it is an infernal blot on the very face of our immaculate constitution, I cannot avoid expressing my surprise that when you recommended our form of government as a model, you did not caution the French against the arbitrary custom of pressing men for the sea service. You should have hinted to them, that property in England is much more secure than liberty, and not have concealed that the liberty of an honest mechanic–his all–is often sacrificed to secure the property of the rich. For it is a farce to pretend that a man fights for his country, his hearth, or his altars, when he has neither liberty nor property. –His property is in his nervous arms–and they are compelled to pull a strange rope at the surly command of a tyrannic boy, who probably obtained his rank on account of his family connections, or the prostituted vote of his father, whose interest in a borough, or voice as a senator, was acceptable to the minister.

Our penal laws punish with death the thief who steals a few pounds; but to take by violence, or trepan, a man, is no such heinous offence.–For who shall dare to complain of the venerable vestige of the law that rendered the life of a deer more sacred than that of a man? But it was the poor man with only his native dignity who was thus oppressed–and only metaphysical sophists and cold mathematicians can discern this insubstantial form; it is a work of abstraction–and a gentleman of lively imagination must borrow some drapery from fancy before he can love or pity a man. —Misery, to reach your heart, I perceive, must have its cap and bells; your tears are reserved, very naturally considering your character, for the declamation of the theatre, or for the downfall of queens, whose rank alters the nature of folly, and throws a graceful veil over vices that degrade humanity; whilst the distress of many industrious mothers, whose helpmates have been torn from them, and the hungry cry of helpless babes, were vulgar sorrows that could not move your commiseration, though they might extort an alms. 'The tears that are shed for fictitious sorrow are admirably adapted,' says Rousseau, 'to make us proud of all the virtues which we do not possess.'

The baneful effects of the despotic practice of pressing we shall, in all probability, soon feel; for a number of men, who have been taken from their daily employments, will shortly be let loose on society, now that there is no longer any apprehension of a war.

Letters Written in France
(1790)

Helen Maria Williams (1762-1827)

I ARRIVED at Paris, by a very rapid journey, the day before the Federation; and when I am disposed to murmur at the evils of my destiny, I shall henceforth put this piece of good fortune into the opposite scale, and reflect how many disappointments it ought to counterbalance. Had the packet which conveyed me from Brighton to Dieppe sailed a few hours later; had the wind been contrary; in short, had I not reached Paris at the moment I did reach it, I should have missed the most sublime spectacle which, perhaps, was ever represented on the theatre of this earth.

I shall send you once a week the details which I promised when we parted, though I am well aware how very imperfectly I shall be able to describe the images which press upon my mind. It is much easier to feel what is sublime, than to paint it; and all I shall be able to give you will be a faint sketch, to which your own imagination must add colouring and spirit. The night before the Federation, by way of prelude to the solemnities of that memorable day, the Te Deum was performed at the church of Notre Dame, by a greater number of musicians than have ever been assembled together, excepting at Westminster Abbey. The Overture which preceded the Te Deum was simple and majestic; the music, highly expressive, had the power of electrifying the hearers: and near the conclusion of the piece, the composer, by artful discords, produced a melancholy emotion; and then, by exciting ideas of trouble and inquietude, prepared the mind for a recitative which affected the audience in a very powerful manner, by recalling the images of that consternation and horror which prevailed in Paris on the 13th of July, 1789, the day before that on which the Bastille was taken. The words were, as well as I can recollect, what follows:—"People, your enemies advance, with hostile sentiments, with menacing looks! They come to bathe their hands in your blood! Already they encompass the walls of your city! Rise, rise from the inaction in which you are plunged, seize your arms, and fly to the combat! God will combat with you!" These words were succeeded by a chorus of instruments and voices, deep and solemn, which seemed to chill the soul. But what completed the effect was, when the sound of a loud and heavy bell mixed itself with this awful concert, in imitation of the alarm-bell, which, the day before the taking of the Bastille, was rung in every church and convent in Paris; and which, it is said, produced a confusion of sounds inexpressibly horrible. At this moment the audience appeared to breathe with difficulty; every heart seemed frozen with terror: till at length the bell ceased, the music changed its tone, and another recitative announced the entire defeat of the enemy; and the whole terminated, after a flourish of drums and trumpets, with an hymn of thanksgiving to the Supreme Being.

I Promised to send you a description of the Federation; but it is not to be described! One must have been present, to form any judgment of a scene, the sublimity of which depended much less on its external magnificence than on the effect it produced on the minds of the spectators. "The people, sure, the people were the sight!" I may tell you of pavilions, of triumphal arches, of altars on which incense was burnt, of two hundred thousand men walking in procession; but how am I to give you an adequate idea of the behaviour of the spectators? How am I to paint the impetuous feelings of that immense, that exulting multitude? Half a million of people assembled at a spectacle, which furnished every image that can elevate the mind of man; which connected the enthusiasm of moral sentiment with the solemn pomp of religious ceremonies; which addressed itself at once to the imagination, the understanding, and the heart!

The Champ de Mars was formed into an immense amphitheatre; round which were erected forty rows of seats, raised one above another with earth, on which wooden forms were placed. Twenty days labour, amimated by the enthusiasm of the people, accomplished what seemed to require the toil of years. Already in the Champ de Mars the distinctions of rank were forgotten; and, inspired by the same spirit, the highest and lowest orders of citizens gloried in taking up the spade, and assisting the persons employed in a work on which the common welfare of the State depended. Ladies took the instruments of labour in their hands, and removed a little of the earth, that they might be able to boast that they also had assisted in the preparations at the Champ de Mars; and a number of old soldiers were seen voluntarily bestowing on their country the last remains of their strength. A young Abbé of my acquaintance told me, that the people beat a drum at the door of the convent where he lived, and obliged the Superior to let all the Monks come out, and work in the Champ de Mars. The Superior with great reluctance acquiesced: "Quant à moi," said the young Abbé, "je ne demandois pas mieux.."

At the upper end of the amphitheatre a pavilion was built for the reception of the King, the Queen, their attendants, and the National Assembly, covered with striped tent-cloth of the national colours, and decorated with streamers of the same beloved tints, and fleurs de lys. The white flag was displayed above the spot where the King was seated. In the middle of the Champ de Mars *l'Autel de la Patrie* was placed, on which incense was burnt by priests dressed in long white robes, with sashes of national ribbon. Several inscriptions were written on the altar; but the words visible at the greatest distance were, "La Nation, la Loi, & le Roi.."

At the lower end of the amphitheatre, opposite to the pavilion, three triumphal arches were erected, adorned with emblems and allegorical figures.

The procession marched to the Champ de Mars, through the central streets of Paris. At La Place de Louis Quinze, the escorts, who carried the colours, received under their banners, ranged in two lines, the National Assembly, who came from the Tuilleries. When the procession passed the street where Henry the Fourth was assassinated, every man paused as if by general consent: the cries of joy were suspended, and succeeded by a solemn silence. This tribute of regret, paid from the sudden impulse of feeling at such a moment, was perhaps the most honourable testimony to the virtues of that amiable Prince which his memory has yet received.

In the streets, at the windows, and on the roofs of the houses, the people, transported with joy, shouted and wept as the procession passed. Old men were seen kneeling in the streets, blessing God that they had lived to witness that happy moment. The people ran to the doors of their houses, loaded with refreshments, which they offered to the troops; and crowds of women surrounded the soldiers, and holding up their infants in their arms, and melting into tears, promised to make their children imbibe, from their earliest age, an inviolable attachment to the principles of the new constitution.

The procession entered the Champ de Mars by a long road, which thousands of people had assisted in forming, by filling up deep hollows, levelling the rising grounds, and erecting a temporary bridge across the Seine, opposite to the triumphal arches. The order of the procession was as follows:

A troop of horse, with trumpets.
A great band of music.
A detachment of grenadiers.
The electors chosen at Paris in 1789.
A band of volunteers.
The assembly of the representatives of the people.
The military committee.
Company of chasseurs.
A band of drums.
The Presidents of sixty districts.
The Deputies of the people sent to the Federation.
The Administrators of the Municipality.
Bands of music and drums.
Battalion of children, carrying a standard, on which was written, *L'Espérance de la Patrie* -.
Detachment with the colours of the national guard of Paris.
Battalion of veterans.
Deputies from forty-two departments, arranged alphabetically.
The Oriflamme, or grand standard of the Kings of France.
Deputies from the regular troops.

Deputies from the navy.
Deputies from forty-one departments.
arranged also alphabetically.
Band of volunteer chasseurs.
Troop of horse, with trumpets.

The procession, which was formed with eight persons abreast, entered the Champ de Mars beneath the triumphal arches, with a discharge of cannon. The deputies placed themselves round the inside of the amphitheatre. Between them and the seats of the spectators, the national guard of Paris were ranged; and the seats round the amphitheatre were filled with four hundred thousand people. The middle of the amphitheatre was crowded with an immense multitude of soldiers. The National Assembly walked towards the pavilion, where they placed themselves with the King, the Queen, the Royal Family, and their attendants; and opposite this group, rose in perspective the hills of Passy and Chaillot, covered with people. The standards, of which one was presented to each department of the kingdom, as a mark of brotherhood, by the citizens of Paris, were carried to the altar, to be consecrated by the bishop. High mass was performed, after which Monsieur de la Fayette, who had been appointed by the King Major-General of the Federation, ascended the altar, gave the signal, and himself took the national oath. In an instant every sword was drawn, and every arm lifted up. The King pronounced the oath, which the President of the National Assembly repeated, and the solemn words were reechoed by six hundred thousand voices; while the Queen raised the Dauphin in her arms, shewing him to the people and the army. At the moment the consecrated banners were displayed, the sun, which had been obscured by frequent showers in the course of the morning, burst forth; while the people lifted their eyes to heaven, and called upon the Deity to look down and witness the sacred engagement into which they entered. A respectful silence was succeeded by the cries, the shouts, the acclamations of the multitude: they wept, they embraced each other, and then dispersed.

You will not suspect that I was an indifferent witness of such a scene. Oh, no! this was not a time in which the distinctions of country were remembered. It was the triumph of human kind; it was man asserting the noblest privilege of his nature; and it required but the common feelings of humanity, to become in that moment a citizen of the world. For myself, I acknowledge that my heart caught with enthusiasm the general sympathy; my eyes were filled with tears; and I shall never forget the sensations of that day, 'while memory holds her seat in my bosom.'

The weather proved very unfavourable during the morning of the Federation; but the minds of people were too much elevated by ideas of moral good, to attend to the physical evils of the day. Several heavy showers were far from interrupting the general gaiety. The people, when drenched by the rain, called out, with exultation, rather than regret, — 'Nous sommes mouillés à la nation.' Some exclaimed, — 'La révolution Françoise est cimenté avec de l'eau, au lieu de sang.' The national guard, during the hours which preceded the arrival of the procession, amused the spectators ‡ d'une dance ronde, and with a thousand whimsical and playful evolutions, highly expressive of that gaiety which distinguishes the French character. I believe none but Frenchmen would have diverted themselves, and half a million of people, who were waiting in expectation of a scene the most solemn upon record, by circles of ten thousand men galloping ‡ en dance ronde. But if you are disposed to think of this gaiety with the contempt of superior gravity, for I will not call it wisdom, recollect that these dancers were the very men whose bravery formed the great epocha of French liberty; the heroes who demolished the towers of the Bastille, and whose fame will descend to the latest posterity.

Such was the admirable order with which this august spectacle was conducted, that no accident interrupted the universal festivity. All carriages were forbidden during that day, and the entrances to the Champ de Mars were so numerous, that half a million of people were collected together without a crowd.

The people had only one subject of regret; they murmured that the King had taken the national oath in the pavilion, instead of performing that ceremony at the foot of the altar; and some of them, crowding round Mons. de la Fayette, conjured him to persuade the King to go to the altar, and take the oath a second time. ⁻ 'Mes enfans,' said Mons. de la Fayette, 'le serment n'est pas une ariette, on ne peut pas le jouer deux fois.'

Mons. de la Fayette, after the Federation, went to the Château de la Muette, where a public dinner was prepared for the national guard. An immense crowd gathered round him when he alighted from his horse, at a little distance from the château; and some Aristocrates, mixing themselves with the true worshippers of him who is so justly the idol of the French nation, attempted to stifle him with their embraces. He called out, "⁻ *Mais, mes amis, vous m'étouffez!*" and one of his *aides de camp,* who perceived the danger of his general, threw himself from his horse, which he entreated Mons. de la Fayette to mount. He did so, and hastened to the château.

This incident reminds me of a line in Racine's fine tragedy of Britannicus, where Nero says,

‡J'embrasse mon rival, mais c'est pour l'étouffer.

Adieu.

Bibliography

Blake, William. "The French Revolution. A Poem in Seven Bools."
    Literature Online. Prophetic Works, Unengraved, 1965.
    Literature Online. Web. 30 Sept. 2014.

Blakemore, Steven. *Crisis in representation : Thomas Paine, Mary
    Wollstonecraft, Helen Maria Williams, and the rewriting of
    the French Revolution*. Madison: Fairleigh Dickinson
    University Press, 1997. Print.

Burke, Edmund, and J.C.D. (Editor) Clark. *Reflections on the
    Revolution in France*. Stanford: Stanford University Press,
    2001. Print.

Butler, Marilyn, ed. *Burke, Paine, Godwin and the Revolution
    Controversy*. New York: Cambridge University Press, 1984.
    Print.

Godwin, William. *Enquiry Concerning Political Justice and its
    Influence on Morals and Happiness*. Toronto: University of
    Toronto Press, 1969. Print.

Kennedy, Deborah. *Helen Maria Williams and the Age of Revolution*.
    Lewisburg: Bucknell University Press, 2002. Print.

Lock, F.P. *Edmund Burke, 1729-1797*. New York: Oxford University
    Press, 1998. Print.

Marshall, Peter H. *William Godwin*. New Haven: Yale University
    Press, 1984. Print.

Moore, Jane. *Mary Wollstonecraft*. Plymouth, U.K.: Northcote House,
    1999. Print.

Nelson, Craig. *Thomas Paine : enlightenment, revolution, and the birth of modern nations*. New York: Viking, 2006. Print.

Paley, Morton D. *William Blake*. Oxford: Phaidon Press, 1978. Print.

Peach, W. Bernard, and D.O. Thomas, eds. *The Correspondence of Richard Price*. Durham: Duke University Press, 1983. Print.

Price, Richard. *A Discourse on the Love of Our Country*. London: Edward E. Powars, Court Street, 1790. *American Antiquarian Society and NewsBank, inc.*. Web. 30 Sept. 2014.

Shusterman, Noah C. *The French Revolution : faith, desire, and politics*. London ; New York: Routledge, Taylor & Francis Group, 2014. Print.

Williams, Helen Maria. *Letters from France*. Boston: J. Belknap and A. Young, 1792. *American Antiquarian Society and NewsBank, inc.*. Web. 29 Sept. 2014.

Wollstonecraft, Mary. *A Vindication of the Rights of Men*. Amherst: Prometheus Books, 1996. Print.

Young, Arthur. *Arthur Young's Travels In France During the Years 1787, 1788, 1789*. London: Bell and Sons, 1909. *Hathi Trust Digital Library*. Web. 4 Oct. 2014.

Young, Arthur. *The Example of France, a Warning to Britain*. London: W. Richardson, 1794. *Hathi Trust Digital Library*. Web. 1 Oct. 2014.